Writing the Land: Wanderings I

Writing the Land: Wanderings I
Edited by Lis McLoughlin

Published by NatureCulture LLC
www.nature-culture.net
www.writingtheland.org

ISBN: 978-1-960293-05-3
First Edition

Cover Artwork: *Lunar XIII* by Martin Bridge
www.thebridgebrothers.com
Cover design: Christopher Gendron and Lis McLoughlin
Interior book design: Lis McLoughlin

Other books in this series:
Writing the Land: Virginia (2024)
Writing the Land: Wanderings II (2024)
Writing the Land: The Connecticut River (2023)
Writing the Land: Currents (2023)
Writing the Land: Channels (2023)
Writing the Land: Streamlines (2023)
Writing the Land: Youth Write the Land (2023)
Writing the Land: Foodways and Social Justice (2022)
Writing the Land: Windblown I (2022)
Writing the Land: Windblown II (2022)
Writing the Land: Maine (2022)
Writing the Land: Northeast (2021)
For more information: www.nature-culture.net

Writing the Land: Wanderings I

Edited by Lis McLoughlin
Foreword by Patrick Curry

Published by
NatureCulture LLC
Northfield, MA

Let me try to name some of the processes at work in this book....

One we might call animism. By this I mean the practice of recognizing and honoring the living land, and refusing to see nature as a dead commodity, a resource which can then be manipulated without any ethical considerations, solely for the benefit of a small subsection of humanity.

Another key aspect of the anthology is openness to Indigenous land guardianship and traditional ecological knowledge: the precious wisdom resulting from centuries of living in place and with place, and the practices that result.

A third dimension is green education. The opportunity for children and young adults to experience the natural world on its own terms, unmediated by a screen, in the company of those who can knowledgeably and respectfully introduce it to them, is absolutely essential. How else can they learn to personally appreciate its delicacy as well as strength, and its evolutionary and ecological dynamics, which must otherwise remain dangerously abstract?

Finally, there is art: the moving, touching and funny poems and photographs celebrating all natural beings, from humans to non-human animals of all kinds, plants, trees, rocks, soil, places and moments; celebrating but also, inseparably, elegizing their passing away. For art grows out of our lives as Earthlings, and will eventually – like the rest of us and what we do – return to the Earth. So it is only fitting that art should address it, reminding us that we are never separate from nature.

Together, these processes add up to a deep common thread of ecocentrism: an understanding that the more-than-human natural world is the ultimate source and terminus of all value. That understanding includes humans as part of the natural world, but rejects the limiting of its value to the strictly human world. Overall they convey a profound sense of hope, which seems to be in short supply these days.

Photo (opposite): Storm Over Mountain by Marty Espinola

Yet beyond this common core of respect for nature, there are differences among the chapters as well, and paying attention to them brings another dynamic to light.

Edges and boundaries in the natural world, where one kind of habitat and the life it supports meets another, are often places of the greatest biodiversity. By analogy, it seems to me that where animism/land agency, Indigenous wisdom, green education and art all meet and mingle is precisely where the greatest degree of cultural diversity obtains, including opportunities for the ecocentric virtues here expressed. This book creates a liminal place where solidarity and learning come to the fore, because no single party is in charge. By the same token there is no tyranny of 'the right position', only the more important question: are we moving in a good direction? So, long and deep may these land conservation trusts (and others) flourish! For all our sakes.

—Patrick Curry, PhD
The Ecological Citizen, Editor-in-Chief
London, England

Our Quiet Chorus
by Jim Minick

We write the land and the land writes us
a resurrection letter posted every day,
the music of mycelium our quiet chorus.

The skin between us stretches thin and porous.
Maples know this and so does clay
if we write the land and the land writes us.

What is a word? Language limited, yet raucous,
a finger pointing, wild tongue-play.
Always, the miracle of mycelium a quiet chorus.

If Earth suddenly was minus us,
would it rejoice or mourn or simply say
we forgot to write, so the land stopped writing us?

A volcano dances with fire's mad rush,
and lava flows like water over all that we say.
Eventually, mycelium returns to sing its chorus.

Like it or not, the land will survive us.
The last supper will be heaven to a worm and a jay.
Still, if we write the land, the land might right us,
and a mouthful of mycelium will be our quiet chorus.

Photo: Mushroom Bunch in Woods by Marty Espinola

WRITING THE LAND: WANDERINGS I
TABLE OF CONTENTS

PRESUMPSCOT REGIONAL LAND TRUST

Presumpscot Regional Land Trust

Maine

The Presumpscot Regional Land Trust engages with communities to conserve, steward, and provide access to local lands and clean water for current and future generations to enjoy.

-Hawkes Preserve
    -Poet: Lisa Hibl
    -School Partner: Great Falls Elementary School
        Allie Rimkunas, Art teacher, and her students

Presumpscot Regional Land Trust

Presumpscot Regional Land Trust is a community-based nonprofit serving Gorham, Gray, Standish, Westbrook, and Windham. We hold conserved lands with free public access preserves that include trails and water access. We are the water stewards of the Presumpscot River watershed and we coordinate the Sebago to the Sea Trail, a 28-mile trail from Standish to Portland.

We are nationally accredited by the Land Trust Accreditation Commission. To learn more about our vision and long term plans see our Strategic Plan.

We envision a future where:

- Networks of conserved land, clean water, wildlife habitat, working farms, and public access to nature are recognized as vital assets to the economy and quality of place.

- People of all ages are connected to the outdoors and the next generation is inspired to be environmental stewards.

Hawkes Preserve by Brenna Crothers

Presumpscot
Regional
Land Trust

Hawkes Preserve
Gorham, ME

The Hawkes Preserve has two trailheads.
The main trailhead is at the end of Towpath Road,
which is off of Route 202 in Gorham.
There is also a trailhead along the northern parking
lot of Great Falls Elementary School.

TRAIL DISTANCE
The full trail loop is 1.2

Preserve Boundaries
Story Walk Trail
Loop Trail
Trailheads
Paddle Access
Contours (20 feet)
Scavenger Hunt Points

0   125 250   500
Feet

End of Towpath Section
End of Story Walk

Presumpscot River

Cumberland-Oxford Canal Towpath

Fairy & Gnome Village

Private
Property

Route 202

Depot St

Private
Property

Story Walk Begins Here

**Great Falls
Elementary School**

N

Tow Path Rd

(202)

Presumpscot Regional Land Trust supports healthy lands, waters, wildlife, and people across the
Presumpscot River watershed through conservation, water quality monitoring, education, and public
access. Our success is based on member support. To learn more and become a member go to www.prlt.org.

Hawkes Preserve

Hawkes Preserve is located in Gorham Maine. There is a 1-mile nature loop trail on the Preserve, which includes several stops to learn more about the natural area. The trail winds through hemlock forests, along the scenic Presumpscot River and follows along the historic Cumberland and Oxford Canal. The Cumberland and Oxford Canal was built to move products from western Maine to the port of Portland and roughly followed the Presumpscot River from Sebago Lake through Standish, Windham, Gorham and Westbrook. This easy trail along the Presumpscot River includes a few bridges, and is a cool and shady summer hike.

The preserve features a seasonal story walk, which displays a book along the trail with different pages mounted and displayed on posts for readers to enjoy as they walk. The story walk is a fun way to engage families in literacy while being active. The story walk is updated seasonally and is maintained with the help of volunteers and the United Way of Greater Portland.

The Hawkes Preserve is adjacent to the Great Falls Elementary School and the trail can be accessed from the school or Tow Path Road.
- Tow Path Trailhead: At the end of Tow Path Road off Route 202 in Gorham.
- Great Falls School Trailhead: 73 Justice Way, Gorham. Park at the back of the school lot. The trail begins at the bottom of the hill by the school's outdoor classroom.

This Preserve is in the homeland of the Wabanaki People. We respectfully acknowledge these People of the Dawn—past, present and future—and their connection to these lands and waters.

There is no hunting allowed on the Hawkes Preserve and motorized vehicles are not allowed (excluding snowmobiles).

Hawkes Preserve is owned by the Presumpscot Regional Land Trust.

Great Falls Elementary, 2nd Grade
Allie Rimkunas, Art teacher

**Choose a good spot to settle down and sketch.
Then write about your drawing.
What do you see in this outdoor classroom?
What questions do you have here?*

April 10, 2023: A Composite Poem
by Lisa Hibl

62 degrees, clear and sunny

I find it a good flying day

blue sky
a clear atmosphere
moss
branch
log
a stick still as a log
sap on the log

How did this tree fall?

moss green
moving leaves
bugs
a blade of grass
me

Why is the pond so mucky?

bark
stones
rocks
trees
airplanes

Where did the bobcat go and where is its den?

I see cat tails.
I see a fallen tree.

What is that white thing in the sky?

a turtle in the pond
plane lines
a stick with a leaf

Why are there so many crunchy leaves?

Pine trees
dropping their needles

the back of a tree
a turtle sitting

Why is the pond shallow?

because it's so big

Why is the sky so blue?

because all the colors
smash together
in the morning

Great Falls Elementary, 5th Grade
Allie Rimkunas, Art teacher

Partner up. Draw your partner in the foreground and our outdoor classroom in the background. Then write about each. Finally, what do they have in common?

At the Trailhead: A Composite Poem
by Lisa Hibl

April 14, 2023 - 71 degrees and sunny

Lots and
lots of trees
trees in the foreground
and the background.

My friend is sitting peaceful,
the hills taller than the trees.
Both are peacefully waiting to be a star.

Big green sappy trees,
piney smell,
my friend's sweatshirt
green like the grass.

A hill with a house and a dead tree.
Always looking bored all the time
and half asleep
but 100% awesome.

Wet, rough, icy spicy
slaying ticks,
piney, hot, grass,
I am non-speaking tree #8.

My friends are kind and funny and calm.
Nature is as calm right now as my friends.
They are both beautiful.

I can hear a woodpecker bellowing
as crazy as my friends.

My background has everything
that Mrs. R. loves and I love and
the nature that makes a world.

Great Falls Elementary, 5th Grade
Allie Rimkunas, Art Teacher

**A poem built from eavesdropping during the nature walk
led by Brenna Crothers (PRLT), March 29, 2023*

Stick Season

  36 degrees, sunny, cold, calm

What?
I heard a crow.
How did you know it was a crow?
Because at my house we have, like,
a billion. And a white owl in summer.

I saw barks and sticks,
I saw leaves blowing in the wind.
And I heard them.

More deer poop!

This one is hemlock,
this is white pine.

Tons of hemlock tips on the ground.

One time I used my binoculars
to see a porcupine way up high
in a tree.

Did you know that young beech trees can hold their leaves
after death? There's a term for that,
my favorite, "marcescent."

And look right here at these:
these are
little
bitty
hemlock
cones.

PALOUSE LAND TRUST

Idaho

Working with landowners and communities to conserve the lands we love, now and forever, and to enrich connections to the natural world.

Palouse Land Trust helps permanently conserve the very best of the Palouse and north-central Idaho: open spaces and iconic landscapes, rare ecosystems, working farms and forests, healthy wildlife and fish habitat, and special outdoor places that bring the community together.

We envision a future where natural beauty persists, lands are cared for and connected, and healthy soils, wildlife, and clean water are abundant. A place where communities intertwine with the natural world, complementing one another, whether within neighborhoods or on farms, ranches, and forests. A region with an unrivaled quality of life and vibrant economy, where people live knowing that some of the most special places will be protected forever as working lands, preserves, wildlife corridors, and places to recreate or connect with the natural world.

-Dave Skinner Ecological Preserve
    -Poet: Linda Russo
    -Photos: Palouse Land Trust

Palouse Land Trust

Palouse Land Trust was founded in 1995 by a group of citizens concerned about the future of open spaces, wildlife habitat corridors, native ecosystems, and working family farms and forests. Our work is built upon relationships—local people dedicated to the future of this place we cherish for its outstanding beauty and small-town quality of life.

Although the focal area of our work has been in the Palouse and Potlatch River watersheds, our service area spans across the Palouse region of north-central Idaho and southeastern Washington—from the western Bitterroot Range to the scablands of eastern Washington, and from the Camas Prairie to the rugged canyons bounding the Snake River.

Protecting land for open space, wildlife habitat, and ecosystem biodiversity—which directly conserves soil, water, and air quality—will become increasingly challenging as more and more people call north-central Idaho and southeast Washington home. Fragile and highly important habitats like the imperiled Palouse Prairie grasslands and the creeks and wetlands critical to the survival of native fish and birds need protection from the threat of development and land conversion, weed invasion, and the ramifications of a changing climate.

The economic prosperity of our region depends on local working lands where family farming- and forestry-based enterprises are being managed to protect the resources that support a way of life while simultaneously providing environmental benefits.

Accommodating residential and commercial growth while ensuring that the natural environment is protected requires balance and viable, collaborative, and effective organizations with adequate resources and capacity. Palouse Land Trust plans to be there, working in partnership with other conservation organizations, agencies, and local governments.

Dave Skinner Ecological Preserve

With less than 1% of the original habitat remaining, native Palouse Prairie is the most endangered ecosystem in the continental United States. According to early settlers, the rolling hills of the Palouse were once covered with lush fields of native bunchgrasses, hawthorne thickets, wild rose and snowberry, ponderosa pine woodlands, seasonal wetlands with camas as far as the eye could see, and a dizzying array of wildflowers.

Today, native Palouse Prairie exists in small patches of land that were either too rocky or steep to plow for agriculture. These scattered "remnants" are often no larger than an acre or two in size, and isolated from each other by large swaths of farmland. Some plant and animal species have disappeared, and those that remain face a difficult existence.

Home to many rare and special plants and animals like the broad-fruit mariposa lily, Palouse goldenweed, Spalding's catchfly, and the grasshopper sparrow, the 102-acre Dave Skinner Ecological Preserve protects one of the largest and highest quality expanse of native Palouse Prairie left in existence. This special property stretches over the western edge of Paradise Ridge, just south of Moscow, Idaho and will be forever protected so the ecosystem can not only survive, but thrive, for generations to come.

How To Be Native Palouse Prairie
by Linda Russo

return yearly like the perennial you are

allow each plant to move at her own pace
into realization

let some live their whole lives here
let others pass through

refuse instrumentalization
resist industrial modernity's complete colonization

let knowledge traditions find their right forms

offer refuge to goddess, coyote, and catchfly
offer stands of milkweed to monarch butterfly
whose larvae require a food only found in their limbs
offer purple asters to late summer's hungry bees

don't ever feel alone

grant the fair and equitable treatment
of all plant, animal, and human persons

allow their memories and their kin memories to come

host innumerable flowering plants
and their sixteen species of bee kin
allow the netter of flies and the counters of bees
their hours in their fields

make sensible the value of sixteen species of bee kin
and innumerable flowering plants besides

allow the deepening scent of ponderosa pine bark
to mean what's sweetest to those who breathe in

be orbital, ephemeral, ancient, eternal
make the sacred visible to the human eye

admit the impermanence of all
human endeavor

say *it's not just that we were destroyed*
it's that we survive
it's that our survivance brings forth critical knowledge

generate sympathy through your fragile cryptogamic crust
in all whose feet land with unavoidable crunching

let all seekers form deep roots
never let them take the same path twice
help them prepare for what will come

View of Palouse Prairie
for Ave
by Linda Russo

On this ridge
in breath and
breadth –
                    the largest
intact remnant of
native prairie around
here –
          through retired
crop grass we
walked –
               following the
drainage (as farmers say)
to find five camas
in blue-violet bloom –
                              stepping
gently between communities of
cryptogamic crust –
                         cringing at
unavoidable crunch
of moss
and lichen –
               the ancient
redwoods of this biome
(as biologists say) –
                         walking
around mounded
footprints of wind
called *mimas* –
                    not
named for Saturn's
moon but *mimas*
plural –
          the many curves
the eyes crest when
taking the hillside in –

Looking out
over patches and
swirls of croplands
stretching out to horizon
Ave says —
                    I wonder if
we could photoshop
it —
         what if we
take this —
                    she
says, bracketing chirping
buzzing hilltop in
her hands —
                    and
place it over
this —
         she says
rotating west, placing
her frame over
how things are
now —
         to create
one enormous endless
prairie view —

you won't find lilacs
by Linda Russo

on a true native prairie remnant you won't find lilacs, *ventenata,* cell
towers, tarmac, convenience stores, oxeye daisies, highway construction;
won't find inscrutable texts, arcane theories, devious plans; you won't
find *chronos* (blows away with the wind), plastic (for now, you won't find
plastic), cigarette butts (not even weathered cigarette butts); you won't
find domestics, exotics, importing, exporting, the price of beans, all your
debts scattered to the wind; won't find ideologies, salvation, absolution,
apathy; you won't find stillness, how the boulders arrived, how long
they've been mined by lichen; won't find enough ink to write all the
things;

      you won't find grief, but it will find you;

on a true native prairie remnant you will find a hunger growingly slow,
a need to pause, a place to rest, the people you came with, cell phone
reception, green beings, rust yellows, browns, blues, an unobscured cloud
view, a place to pee; a constant music, a lichen archive on a living rock,
flower-like birds, feather-like flowers, a wind dictionary giving you all
the words for how it feels on your skin; branches of pine needles facing
one direction, rusted pails and bedsprings, surfaces moved into new
forgiveness by atmospheric forces; the strength to say goodbye to one
thing that you've carried since before your birth; the warm ponderosa
scent you wanted (you didn't know it would land just so);

next year, glacier lily
next year, grass widows
next year, yellow bells
next year, plant teachers showing how to hold your true head aloft;

you will find these next year
if you arrive with the season of spring snow.

APPALACHIA OHIO ALLIANCE

Ohio

AOA is dedicated to the conservation and stewardship of our land and water as sustainable natural resources that are an asset and a legacy for our community.

-Bison Hollow
    -Poet: Kari Gunter-Seymour[*]
-Lamb Preserve
    -Poet: Scott Woods
-Cedar Run Preserve
    Poet: Su Flatt

[*]NB: Gunter-Seymour's Bison Hollow poems for Appalachia Ohio Alliance were honored by being published in The Anthology of Appalachian Writers, Volume XVI (April, 2024)

Appalachia Ohio Alliance Land Conservancy

The Appalachia Ohio Alliance (AOA) is a regional non-profit land conservancy that operates in central and southern Ohio. AOA is dedicated to the conservation and stewardship of our land and water as sustainable natural resources that are an asset and a legacy for our community. Now in our twenty-second year, AOA has conserved over 15,750 acres in twenty-one counties. We are presently stewarding over 8,400 acres of fee lands and 6,200 acres of lands protected through conservation agreements. Most AOA properties are preserved in a "forever wild" state.

Photo © Steve Fleegal

The Alliance achieves its mission through several principal activities: land and water conservation and stewardship; community outreach; outdoor recreation; nature-based education; and mission advocacy. Through our work we strive to build community awareness, support engagement in land and water conservation, as well as to foster healthier communities and greener, more sustainable lifestyles.

As a land conservancy our primary focus is the conservation and stewardship of land and water resources. These efforts concentrate on multiple priority initiatives to achieve meaningful conservation outcomes. These include the conservation of: valuable and unique natural areas and habitats; riparian zones including riparian-based greenway corridors; working farms and farm lands; community forests; buffer lands surrounding local, state and federal parks and forests; historical and cultural resources; connective corridors of conserved habitat; and larger, landscape-scale assemblages of conservation lands. With all of our conserved properties, AOA seeks to enhance and/or restore the natural features, characteristics and qualities of the land and water resources unique to each site.

AOA employs stewardship staff to help oversee our properties. Supplementing our board and staff is a strong corps of volunteers and trained naturalists who provide guidance, input and assistance to our programs and efforts. We conduct nature-based education and outdoor recreation programs and activities to increase the opportunity for participation and active engagement of the public and local community in conservation.

Photo © Steve Fleegal

Bison Hollow Preserve: One of Ohio's Natural Gems

AOA's Bison Hollow Preserve is one of the jewels of the distinctive and spectacular unglaciated Hocking Hills landscape in southern Ohio. The Preserve is centered on protection of the East Fork of Queer Creek and its headwater tributaries — a Coldwater Habitat aquatic system designated Outstanding State Waters, the highest classification in Ohio.

The primary feature is a narrow, steep-walled Black Hand Sandstone gorge with numerous picturesque natural features. The many high sandstone outcrops and bluffs, side gorges, rock shelters and caves, numerous waterfalls and relatively rare high-quality Coldwater habitat streams, are very worthy of conservation.

Bison Hollow is covered in deep older growth hardwood forests with large stands of hemlock that provide homes for many native species that are becoming increasingly threatened or rare. Wildflower displays carpet the forest floor in spring and summer.

Our conservation actions at Bison Hollow have extended for 15 years, from our acquisition of the 76-acre Harwood property in 2009. Today, Bison Hollow Preserve is comprised of more than 20 tracts and approximately 1,100 acres of largely unfragmented habitat, all acquired from voluntary sellers who supported AOA's vision for conservation of this impressive natural landscape.

Bison Hollow Preserve extends the conserved Hocking Hills geography from Hocking County into Vinton County and provides a physical habitat corridor that connects Ohio's Hocking Hills State Park lands to the Wayne National Forest.

Our efforts at Bison Hollow and elsewhere in the Hocking Hills help compliment and safeguard the previous investments made by the State of Ohio to protect and showcase the priceless Hocking Hills landscapes that are a valuable part of Ohio's ecotourism economy.

Bison Hollow is an important component of our Greater Hocking Hills Conservation Initiative. Through these efforts, AOA has a long-term presence and investment in the conservation of exceptional Hocking Hills landscapes, natural resources, native habitats and rural character. Our commitment dates to our first conservation easement in 2002. AOA will soon surpass 90 properties and over 6,000 acres of conserved lands in the Greater Hocking Hills Region.

Photo © Steve Fleegal

Unfortunately, we recognize that the Hocking Hills Region retains a significant number of potential vulnerabilities and liabilities that threaten the sustainability of its natural resources, habitats and water quality, as well as its viability as a high-quality ecotourism destination.

While AOA has achieved many successes there is much conservation left to accomplish to sufficiently conserve the natural heritage and resources so precious to the Hocking Hills region, creating a permanent legacy for the long-term benefit and enjoyment of us all.

Tucking Into the Backcountry
by Kari Gunter-Seymour

I am punch-drunk
before I get a hundred yards
into that hinterland, chuckle
out loud that I am inside
the woods-wide-web,
no cell phone service,
no GPS, no ding or beep
or breaking news alert,
only the low-pitched purr
of a ticklish breeze.

An avalanche of scents
hitchhike those airways—
the vanilla of sweet grass,
tang of honeysuckle,
spice of root beer
from a downed sassafras.
My nose is leading the way,
compass cased and stowed.

I hide my name inside
other names—grape fern,
spleenwort, wild ginger.
Gnarly roots of hemlock
and black birch hug
rock cliffs, same way
a soaring red-tailed clutches
his dinner, black cohosh
and trout lilies smile upwards,
heads bobbing like nests
of hungry baby birds.

I snuggle among them,
lie back against warm bark,
hat pulled low, listen

to the music—the nasally honk
of a randied tree frog,
cool clicks of creek water,
shush of the pines, having
left the cicadas a few turns back
to discuss worries of the world.

Photo © Steve Fleegal

An Unscheduled Day
by Kari Gunter-Seymour

Let me be unruly, escape while I can,
sneak off grid to this outback—
wooded, feathered and bloomed,

a light sprinkle of rain
sponging the greenery,
speckling my cheeks.

Cricket songs stitch the morning,
Wildflowers boast purple
and ochre, their pollen

a salty dust up on the tongue
as I part a path.
Stickseeds hitchhike my sweater.

I spot a perfect rock beneath
a tuck of pin oak, a flat perch,
moss embossed to cradle my bum.

Sun squeaks a peek between clouds,
ruddy foliage swirls in points of light,
goldfinch flit from stem to branch.

A doe stands lengthways in the ryegrass,
doesn't bother to camouflage,
as if she knows my scent.

Breezes whistle like wisps of memory
inside clusters of hemlock. I look
to the foothills, find comfort in their whispers,

wait for a fragrance to ripple the holler,
marvel as afternoon falls
like leaves into deeper color.

Photo © Scott Birrer

Photo © Kathryn Cubert

Lamb Preserve Contributes to Big Darby Creek Conservation Corridor

The 68-acre Lamb Preserve is an important part of AOA's Big Darby Creek Conservation Corridor Initiative. This Preserve contributes to the conservation and restoration of a continuous riparian corridor of connected bottomland forest habitat and associated uplands along Big Darby Creek.

Lamb Preserve protects over 2,300 linear feet of riparian corridor along Big Darby Creek and another 2,400 linear feet of headwater tributary stream. The largely forested site is located on a high bluff along the Big Darby with spectacular wildflower beds that coat the slopes and bottoms each spring. The dense beds of white Trout Lilies are particularly spectacular.

Big Darby Creek is classified as both an Ohio State Scenic River and as a National Wild and Scenic River System that is recognized as one of the most biologically diverse waterways in the Midwest. The Nature Conservancy has designated Big Darby Creek as one of the "Last Great Places" within the Western Hemisphere. It is classified by Ohio EPA as an Exceptional Warmwater Habitat and as Outstanding State Waters.

AOA has now preserved over 1,350 acres along the Big Darby. These properties are a critical component of AOA's efforts to safeguard water quality, natural habitat for native species and the scenic qualities of Big Darby Creek.

The Big Darby Creek corridor is known to harbor a plethora of rare and endangered species including numerous mussels, fish and bats. The Lamb Preserve conserves important aquatic, riparian and upland habitats that are home to numerous species of listed, threatened and/or endangered freshwater fish and mussels, and well as forest habitat suitable for endangered Indiana Bats which have maternity trees along the Big Darby.

The Prodigal Lamb
by Scott Woods

I do not have the sea;
I have you.
Spring rolling in waves of wildflowers
And dragonflies that know a city boy
when they see one,
slipping along the creek
I have been warned I would need a cane for,

And speaking of canes, it makes sense
that solace would find me here,
sheep led onto the trail.
I am the only lamb to be found here,
so preserve me like you do this forest.

I must apologize for leaving
all this me in you.
The river of the city rushes out of me
Into a stream I haven't even
introduced myself to yet,
a tributary of concrete and sirens kissing
the bleating ripples of wind on wetland.

I am sure there is a religion here
somewhere in this field of wildflower,
a blanket or psalm, where a lost lamb
is welcome, held high even,
before being sacrificed to a prodigal child.
Which begs the question, am I the sacrifice or the son?
And when was this knife entered into me?
And why is my mouth filled with roiling spring?

Dominion
by Scott Woods

There is a thing I understand about racists:
how they love their land.
How their homes become empires
even when the acreage is small.

All of the places that my family comes from,
that I grew up visiting or sleeping in
or eating in, are lost to me.
Sold or handed away or demolished.
The rooms that I could not appreciate
when I was a child stick
to my memory, the silt of my impression
ground from every potato chip bag
and picnic plate soiled with a god's potato salad.

The liminal intertwining of the human and nonhuman
cannot be avoided here.
I recognize the necessity of its preservation.
I contend with the nonhuman every day.
Ask me again about my hair,
blooming wild this season too,
pined for, irresistible to the touch.
And doesn't something die every day out here, too?

I have carved my name into the side of a weed here,
where all the flowers are too wild for signatures.
Turns out I, too, can be an invasive species.
I claim this part, this unclaimable
unasked-for rag of beauty
that I can name in three notes of a songbird,
before anyone realizes it's missing.

Photo (above) © Jenny Adkins
Photo (below) © Steve Fleegal

Cedar Run Watershed Conservation

Cedar Run is a relatively small watershed in the Mad River Valley which is home to one of the most valued and unique natural areas in Ohio – Cedar Bog State Nature Preserve. There are numerous rare, threatened and/or endangered species in the Cedar Run watershed - virtually all of which are concentrated in Cedar Bog, which contains a rare and unique remnant wetland ecosystem, that has been eradicated from surrounding areas.

Named for the relict population of northern white cedar, Cedar Run receives most of its water from cold water springs fed by a continuous flow of groundwater arising from underground glacially influenced geologic formations. This condition creates a microenvironment which supports a diverse and relatively unique ecosystem that is vulnerable to external forces.

The resiliency and sustainability of the habitats in Cedar Bog are highly dependent on the maintenance of the current groundwater level. The unique habitats and plant associations found here were once widespread but are now confined to a small wetland "island" with no connectivity to other natural systems. As the many wetland habitats that once graced the region have disappeared, flora and fauna that were once relatively common have become rare, while those that were rare have become endangered or extirpated.

AOA is pursuing strategic actions to conserve and protect the rare and unique habitats in the Cedar Run watershed, and the conditions that allow them to exist. As part of a long term, landscape scale conservation approach, AOA seeks to: protect and restore riparian areas of Cedar Run and adjacent properties that are suitable to be returned to wetland and other comparable and compatible habitats, expanding the areas that can support the unique habitats and rare species living in the watershed; help protect and enhance surface and groundwater resources; and provide suitable natural buffers for the unique plant communities. These areas would be connected to and incorporated into the lands that have already been preserved in the watershed.

RE: Wild (Cascade / Cleave)

I sit up straight,
listen carefully, ask questions
well-mannered now, I was wild once
I close my eyes
I can almost remember

Dancing in dirt with white shoes
I believe, I can talk to some squirrels,
and all plants. I carry rocks in my pockets
I don't hear mama call. I'm dancing
Set the table and wash up
I sit up straight

Like a grown up, I forget
my elbows, wiggle too much,
reach too far, laugh too loudly,
receive strong reminders to settle
listen closely, ask questions

Why why why questions, why
be still? Why clean our plates
when we're already full? I'm
told to "settle, eat, know my place"
well-mannered now,
I was wild once.

All body, voice, opinion, open
eager explorer, adventuring
into everything vast and strange
Drawn in line by rules and rulers, measured
I close my eyes

I see electric fire purples
turning the tired bland and beige
they wrapped me in to rainbows
I can almost remember.

by Su Flatt

Searching for the signs
of the path, almost invisible,
watching, wandering, finally
seek the seeds of wild here
fen, creek, rattlesnake

Beyond the mowed lawn, the world can
grow everything, sedge, cedar, orchid
queen of the prairie, massasaga rattlesnake.
among dense blazing stars
with bubbling water, ready to grow
searching for the signs

The hollow sedges, muck and marl, up to
near the boardwalk, we tread soft, we don't
disturb the balance, the wild harmony
in these few acres of untame,
of the path, almost invisible

How did it shrink? How could we
Always take take take more more more
mixing up need and want, we were
all cultivate and rip up wild, claim land
and 7,000 acres became 130 acres of
watching, wandering, finally

Acres of lush self-sustanance, landbreath,
hemmed in, by straight lines, rows shaped
into unnatural grids, curveless
conquered, contained, consumable
seeks the seeds of wild here

And greens, sprout slow, root in
the old soil, repairing, restoring the earth
reclaiming, rewilding, remembering
Fen, creek, rattlesnake.

Photo © Jenny Adkins

FREEPORT CONSERVATION TRUST

Freeport
Conservation
Trust

Maine

Our mission is to protect, preserve, connect open space lands and provide public access to natural areas in Freeport, Maine, including forests, farmland, scenic vistas, wildlife habitat, and shoreland.

-Frost Gully
    -Poet: Mike Bove
    -Photos: Freeport Conservation Trust unless otherwise noted
-South Freeport Trail System
    -Poet: Jan Bindas-Tenney
    -Photographer: Kelly Sink unless otherwise noted
-Powell Point
    -Poet: Audrey Gidman
    -Photos: Freeport Conservation Trust unless otherwise noted
-East Freeport Trail System
    -Poet: Jefferson Navicky
    -Photographer: Kelly Sink

Freeport Conservation Trust

Founded in 1977, Freeport Conservation Trust (FCT) works to protect its 1,780 acres of property, including scenic farmland, vital shorefront, and vast woodlands in Freeport, Maine. FCT holds permanent restrictions on property through conservation easements or outright ownership and provide public access to natural spaces by building and maintaining trails. Our collaborations aid in fundraising for land acquisition and management, all the while enabling us to promote and educate our community about land conservation efforts.

The Stewardship, Land and Outreach programs are the core programs at FCT. With an incredibly small staff, we balance maintaining our 25 miles of trails, opening a new trail/property every year, promoting and improving the annual Freeport Trail Challenge for all ages, and increasing opportunities to learn about Freeport's outdoors. Key components to our continued success include our stewardship program which utilizes our talented staff, volunteers, and business partners to maintain and create trail systems for all people to access. FCT hosts educational, free events open to the public to share about the environment and important ecosystems conserved in Freeport.

Frost Gully

Frost Gully is a 13.14 acres of undeveloped land that FCT conserved in 2009. This landlocked parcel was owned by the Freeport water system for 118 years serving as resource protection for the original source of the town's public water supply. The parcel was once part of a much larger tract that was severed when I-295 was constructed. Maine Water retains the portion lying east of the highway. This parcel is comprised of rolling woodlands, small streams, a brook, wetlands, and a pond.

In 2023, FCT and partners embarked upon the removal of three dams-a project that involved 7 years of planning. This collaboration was made possible by partnering with US Fish and Wildlife, Merrymeeting Chapter of Trout Unlimited, Casco Bay Estuary Partnership, and Trout Unlimited. This project has involved extensive invasive species management and reintroduction of native plants. The objective was to enhance the health and interconnectedness of the brook, bolstering the populations of indigenous fish species such as "sea run" and "resident" Wild Eastern Brook Trout, promoting biodiversity. Learn more about this incredible project on our website.

Frost Gully at Season's End
by Mike Bove

Autumn devours us, walking
trails beneath golden overhang.

Do you ever think about the land
before we came, oaks and pines

in towering quiet? Remember
the riddle about whether or not

a falling tree makes noise
if no one is there to hear? Here

it's easy to believe these trees
will never fall, canopy tops

stretched toward the sun, saved
in this place long after we've

gone, followed by others walking
below, looking above, asking

about the trees in hushed
reverence of their silent sounds.

Inheritance
by Mike Bove

Riches of leaf littler blown
near stones at the edge

of the stream. Blue and green
in the bark-moss of shaded

firs. And these, the formless
echoes of those we love,

taken with us always.

Photo (above): Mushrooms by Kelly Sink

Directions & History
by Mike Bove

Erasure poem of Freeport Conservation Trust's website description
of Frost Gully Woods

off   Durham Rd

right as you are

the entrance

is on the left edge   is a small area

you have to drive down

to the left   to get to

        a gift

undeveloped land   is

        the original source

rolling woodlands   small streams

a brook wetlands   a pond

together

these   parcels

protect

South Freeport Trail System

This network of trails totals approximately 5 miles, with the main
network being Bliss Woods. These trails take you through various forest
types and a field loop. There are three access points, including one
from the village of South Freeport. Trails here include: Bliss Woods,
Stonewood, Sayles Field, and Ridge Trail.

I Become a Dewy Wind
After Mónica Gomery
by Jan Bindas-Tenney

Walking on trails
in this in-between wood

by someone's road
I don't know, my neck

a knot of
worry and distraction

its grain wound tightly at the base of
my skull.

Is this belonging?
The way I become a dewy wind

while trudging elastic
through brown leaves.

On a bog bridge
one foot on either side

I float adrift, a flake
in this tentative first snow

in this gully of ferns, an ice pellet
reverberating on dehydrated leaves.

Small streams who collide
and connect the water flows

bring us a season of safety
bring us to the sea.

Meet me on this trail between
binaries, where we can be among

the greens and browns, sweaty and full. Praise how
we slide home, fly overhead, praise loud geese

shouting out - Is this belonging? Ravines
of fallen logs, pine needle beds,

in this audience of timber
I unravel, a small revelation

an ovation of kindling.

Whippoorwill Woods
After Ada Limón
by Jan Bindas-Tenney

Past the outlet malls, past the renovated farmhouses,
past the quaint restaurants, past the scenic coastline,
past the shallow bogs, to get to these woods
named for a bird I heard nearly every night
as a child, a bird I heard as a teen as I walked through dark trees,
as I felt the summer breeze, stared at the moon through
my window screen.
Some say a death omen, a soul stealer type of bird.
I strain to hear, turn my head sideways, where are you, whip-poor-will?
The distant sound of cars, wood chopping, the rush of stream, the falling
rain, maybe the distant ocean waves, other squawking shore birds.
I do not hear the whip and whirl, the swoop and trill.
I do not hear a gape moth-hunter.
Oh, blasting bird of sing-song night call
Is it true? Can you not nestle in the decreasing understory, in the empty
thicket of shrubs cleared clean? Do fewer insects swoop at night?
Is it true?
The malls and highway, the renovations and restaurants,
And now I do not hear your call
Oh, Whip-poor-will, whip-poor-will
What omen? What souls left unstolen?

Woods Meditations During a Catastrophe
After Cameron Awkward Rich
by Jan Bindas-Tenney

Another dark morning and I am spinning. During a catastrophe, I go outside to the woods, to this short lollipop trail, to this trail that leads to other trails, that leads to nowhere, that leads me back to where I started, and I am spinning. I go to these woods in the too cold, in the too hot, and I find any woods, I find the woods of my home, I find the woods in my head, and I am spinning. I try to hear the crunch of lichened branches under foot, try to look at the birch trees against an ochre sky, try to find the red-bellied woodpecker who churrs and drums overhead, and I am spinning. The gathering of wood ferns, the bouquet of wood stove smoke, the fungal ground frill, the mourners in the basilica, the children dead and buried under rubble, and the old farm truck's rusted and broken fender emerges from a downy blanket of jewelweed and wild sarsaparilla, all of it and I am spinning. All of it and a warning sign, *wear blaze orange* or someone walking with a gun may mistake you for a fawn, for a fighter. There's a dream in which I can feel my body moving in these woods. There is no separation like a mycelial filigree. There are no airstrikes or assault rifles, only hands and moss covered logs. Like you, I have a body. Like you, I have children who look at my face in the still dark morning, searching. Hand on my body. Hand on this beech tree trunk. Hand on this broken beech tree trunk.

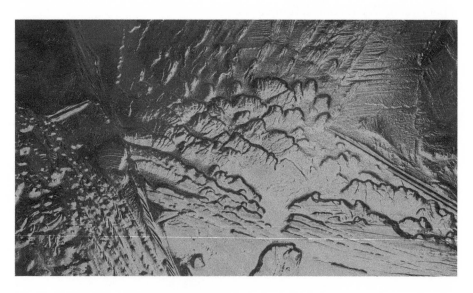

Powell Point

Powell Point is a 29 acre preserve at the mouth of Cousins River. FCT maintains one short (0.8 mile), wooded trail here that loops through knolls of tall pines, ferns, and mossy woods ending with spectacular views on a lookout over Casco Bay.

The Casco Bay watershed (985 square miles) has a rich cultural history and environmental significance. FCT has conserved 195 acres around the Cousins river marsh, protecting 13 parcels upstream from Powell Point, ensuring the shoreline remains undeveloped and will continue to support the movement of the marsh as sea level rises.

Casco Bay is a place with many names. The Wabanaki called this place *Aucocisco* [ah-coh-sis-ko] which can be translated as, "Place of the Herons", or in some accounts, "marshy place" or "place of the slimy mud." The Abanaki word for Great Blue Heron is kasqu'.[1]

Photo (above): Jackman Trail in Fall by Kelly Sink

[1] https://www.cascobay.org/category/community-engagement/casco-bay-curriculum/

Practicing Winter
   Powell Point Preserve, 2023
by Audrey Gidman

How could I forget grief? Look: this tender birch,
steady soil. Little holes left where little things grew.

Look: this ice
ribboning like a lesson in follow-through

between roots I keep falling
into. Look: bruises.

Little bridges. Little stones. Look: ghost
pipe on the path. Little spines.

December, I had to walk a dead end to find you.
I want to know it was worth the trouble.

Look: a place I planted something. A place I didn't.
A forest when I forgot to call it one.

East Freeport Trail System

The East Freeport Trail System is comprised of series of trails leading throughout east Freeport, with views of Kelsey Brook, Mitchell Ledge Farm, Little River, and Maquiot Bay. This trail system includes several individual trails from which various routes can be created. Trails here include, Mitchell Ledge, Kelsey Brook, Brimstone, Gibby's, Antoinette Jackman, Moose Crossing, Tadpole, Forest Ridge and Calderwood.

The Wild Cows of Freeport, Maine
by Jefferson Navicky

I.
When I heard about the cattle shipped from Japan, 10K per cow
coming down the road for their kobe rib-eyes when
their heads roll, when I heard how those cows escaped
my neighbor's pasture made especially for fattening
their marbled flanks, how when given a bit of open air
they'd bolted through a hole in a fence into the forest, disappeared,
when I heard about the search parties through the woods, all this,
I thought, go cows. They've gone free, may they die
in the forest of their own freedom.

II.
Then one day a week later I saw them, or it was like I dreamed I did,
the once-future steaks now free in the forest, all bedded down during
my morning walk with the dog, they looked like a huge fallen tree
in the distant slanted sun until they rose to amble off without even
so much as a bark from the dog, they ambled off legend,
                                        the opposite of ghosts.

III.
I called to report the cows. I thought I was doing my civic, neighborly
duty, I thought the cows couldn't survive long in the woods alone,
weather about to turn, and what about the coyotes? Was there
some buried bias within me that thought new-to-the-country cows
couldn't be hearty enough to survive in the Maine woods? I thought
I was doing the right thing for everyone, cows and people,
but when she heard, my wife said, what do you think is going to
happen to them once they're caught? Does any animal want
the comfort that comes at the price of its own life?

IV.
R. said she visits the cows at Wolfe's Neck Farm to feel calm.
When offered the chance, she didn't want to give a calf a bottle,
she might get too attached. Something about the energy
                                        at which they vibrate.

V.
S., at sixteen years old, leaned her head heavy against the cow's side
as she reached under, both cow and girl almost falling asleep
            during morning milking.

VI.
B., when he milked his first cow on a trip to visit family in a small
village in Ireland, sat beneath its giant rib cage, its rhythm,
            listened to the quiet.

VII.
Later that week when I heard the Japanese cows who ran away
from my neighbor's farm were actually Texas cows raised
on a 15,000-acre ranch where they were used to roaming wild,
when I heard they'd been caught once and returned,
when I heard they'd trampled one pasture fence and jumped another,
when I heard, "that's why it's important we find them soon,"
my neighbor said when I encountered him in the woods looking
for the cows, "if we don't find them soon, we might never,
even if we bring in the dogs." My neighbor the farmer carried
a hiking stick so he could get up and down the gullies, it seemed
only a matter of time before he came upon the cows,
herded them back to whatever home he'd give them for whatever
            time they had left.

VIII.
All next week I had to sit with what I'd done, or at least what
I'd set in motion with my phone call to the farmer. I'd heard no more
news and could only think they'd been caught, remembered
their quiet grace rising from the forest floor.

IX.
Then one morning on my walk with the dog, I crossed a stream
and on the other side was a cow patty the size of a spare tire, fresh
and not more than a few hours old.

X.
Another week, I came up a hill and there they were, four deeply tawny,
almost gold cows staring at me twenty-five yards away and standing
in the middle of the trail like they were out for a casual hike.

Hello cows, and they begin to wag their tails.
My dog barks an excited hello too,
and the cows walk slowly off into memory.

Anonymous Star
by Jefferson Navicky

To the deer spine looped over the tree branch on my woods walk,
I say fuck you and your bone chain. Fuck you little pieces of gristle
still hung on vertebrae like leftover meat not yet flossed by
scavenger's lips. Fuck you the curve, half crescent adjacent,
death with its grappling hooks suspended lunar and more than
a little leering. Your face all teeth. Fuck you
and your wild relief. Your get out of jail free. Proximate and lyrical
I have never died, and don't want to most of the time.
Constellations above me, fuck you and February. Like a star.
Do I need a tether? -- Fine
I choose you to hook me and trail me. Like a star.
Bead me, sit me on your swoop, but beware:
the world hinges on violence and I am no different.

HOWARD COUNTY CONSERVANCY

Maryland

Our mission is to educate children and adults about our natural world, preserve the land and its legacy for future generations, and model responsible stewardship of our environment.

Howard County Conservancy
10520 Old Frederick Road
Woodstock, MD 21163

www.howardnature.org

-Mt. Pleasant
    -Poet: Patti Ross

Mt. Pleasant

For centuries, this land has been shaped by its inhabitants—plant, insect, human or animal. The Howard County Conservancy's Mt. Pleasant farmstead sits high over 232 acres in the lush Patapsco River valley in Howard County, Maryland. We acknowledge and appreciate all those who have passed through or settled on this soil. Here is where we take responsibility for our past, revel in the present and look to the future with hope.

The Past:

> *I love taking nature walks and exploring the grounds as it always reminds me of my childhood time spent on my grandparents' farm ..... I'm so grateful to be a part of enabling the youth of Howard County to also have that experience.*
> — volunteer Carolyn Keaton Culp

Centuries ago, this land was dotted with serpentine barrens, prairies formed on thin, nutrient-poor soil over serpentinite rock. Eastern Woodland Indians stewarded these fields for centuries, burning the brush to clear the ground for hunting elk, deer and rabbit, and gathering its grasses and berries. The most recent tribes to hunt and camp on this land are the Susquehannock and Piscataway/Conoy tribes, who traveled on forest trails, paddled its streams and camped along the Patapsco River. Indigenous people are still here. A researcher who is a member of the Piscataway/Conoy tribe helped the Conservancy compile a more complete history of its land.

In 1692, the colonial government commissioned Thomas Browne, known as the Patuxent Ranger, to survey the lands and keep watch over the activities of the Native Americans. In 1703, Ranger Browne was given a land grant for a 415-acre parcel named Ranter's Ridge, which included the 232 acres the family called Mt. Pleasant.

On that land, at the heart of the Conservancy, eight generations of the Browne/Brown family raised children, livestock and crops. In every census—from the first in the nation in 1790 to emancipation in Maryland in 1864—enslaved people were listed as property by the Brown family and worked this land. One enslaved woman, Kitty Johnson, who turned 16 in 1868, stayed with the Browns as a paid servant long after emancipation.

Ruth and Frances Brown, the last direct descendants of Thomas Browne, lived on the farm all their lives. They taught school, first in a one-room schoolhouse nearby and later in Howard County public schools, for nearly 50 years. Both sisters died without heirs in the early 1990s and asked in their wills to have their property preserved. A community of neighbors gathered to take up the task, and in 1990, the Conservancy formed as a private, nonprofit land trust. In 1993, the trust accepted the gift of Mt. Pleasant.

The historic farmstead includes original outbuildings: a carriage house, blacksmith shop, bank barn, wagon shed, corn crib, smokehouse, chicken coop, guinea fowl coop, ice house foundation and outhouse. A 1700s barn, slated for destruction on another property, was brought, piece by piece, to this property for reconstruction and restoration. For more than 30 years, the Howard County Conservancy has served as steward for the gift of this land.

Photo by Keith Janson

Ranter's Ridge
(erasure poem from the draft writing of the history of Mt. Pleasant)
by Patti Ross

our natural world
land for generations
dedicated
stewardship
ecosystems
animal
plant
life
watershed
educating
232 rolling acres
historic
Susquehannock
Piscataway
Algonquin
all tribes
hunters
wigwams
slave census
in case government
compensate slave owners
Kinsey Johnson, 18, male
Isaac Sheridan, 17, male
Kitty Johnson, 16, female
"now in my employ, shall remain
with and in my family"
Mary Chase, 35, female
Joseph Chase, 14, male
John Chase, 8, male
Joshua Chase, 6, male
Eliza Chase, 2, female
Emily Conway, 4, female
Freedman's Bureau
black farm workers

Photo (above) by David Hobby
Photo (below) by Bonnie Ott

Present:

In this place, may future generations learn a bit about the sacredness of wild places. May they remember the art of listening to the Earth.
— board member Janssen Evelyn

Nature draws people and animals to this land. Lured by the rustle of a warbler at dawn, the early dew on a Community Garden tomato, the delicate ballet of juniper hairstreak butterflies above evergreens or a still, cool forest trail at twilight, visitors flock to this oasis of nature.

More than 40,000 people connect with nature on our land. Sharp eyes have spotted 68 different species of butterfly in one year here. Our resident beaver, fox, deer, owls, viceroy butterflies and bolas spiders are evidence of the biodiversity that is drawn to lands that are stewarded.

We plant native trees and plants, remove invasives, plant meadows and organize clean-ups. A diverse crop of gardeners work plots in our Community Garden, using sustainable practices to grow produce with roots around the world, from corn, squash and okra to long beans and bok choy. Every garden plot contributes labor to tend the area and harvest produce, usually about 4,000 pounds a year, for the local food bank.

And nature nurtures brains here as well, with public environmental education for all ages. We host a pollinator festival in our native plant garden, hikes to spot birds or butterflies, Earth Day service projects and talks by experts on biodiversity, animals, soil and watersheds.

Our gardens, fields, forests and 5 miles of trails are open dawn to dusk daily. All visitors are welcome, free, to our grounds, and can visit our goats, chickens and owls. Our nature center plays host to educational exhibits, including a rescued terrapin and black rat snake. The lands serve as refuge from encroaching suburbia, allowing visitors to both remember the past and envision the future.

Photo (opposite) by Tim Phillips

river prophets
by Patti Ross

a stream runs through
beavers tell the story
hold the water on edge
a berm of perfection
no one noticing until
tree trunks
point upward
precision
beavers understand
take care of the land

Future:

I volunteer at the Conservancy purely for selfish reasons; it fills my cup to see students' eyes alight with knowledge.

           – volunteer Karen Estrada

Children are our future, teach them well and let them lead the way, as the song goes. Connecting young people to nature is essential for their future and for the future of our planet in a climate crisis.

The Conservancy sees the future in the eyes of children discovering the wonders of ice crystals and caterpillars, milkweed seed pods and salamanders.

We offer a Nature Preschool where students are outside nearly every day. Elementary and secondary school field trips allow students to learn about climate justice, biodiversity, amphibians and wetlands. Our summer camp for ages 3 to 12 teaches about plants, birds, water and STEM while offering plenty of outdoor time. The Climate KNOWledge program gets middle-schoolers into the forest to measure trees and learn about food production's effect on climate.

A nationwide Youth Climate Institute offers high school students the chance to work–with hope–on the urgent problem of climate change. The young people learn from environmental scientists, lobby for climate legislation, organize used clothing swaps, plant trees and encourage composting programs.

In addition to welcoming visitors of all ages to its 232 acres, the Conservancy manages more than 2,000 acres of environmentally sensitive land across the county that have been placed in permanent conservation. We're preserving and tending lands on our historic acreage and beyond our property boundaries for generations that haven't yet been born.

Photo by Howard County Conservancy

Map of Mt. Pleasant by Megan Lambert

COASTAL RIVERS CONSERVATION TRUST

**COASTAL RIVERS
CONSERVATION TRUST**

Maine

Coastal Rivers Conservation Trust: Caring for the lands and waters of the Damariscotta-Pemaquid Region by conserving special places, protecting water quality, creating trails and public access, and deepening connections to nature.

-Round Top Farm
        -Poet: Anna M. Drzewiecki
        -Photographer: Hannah McGhee

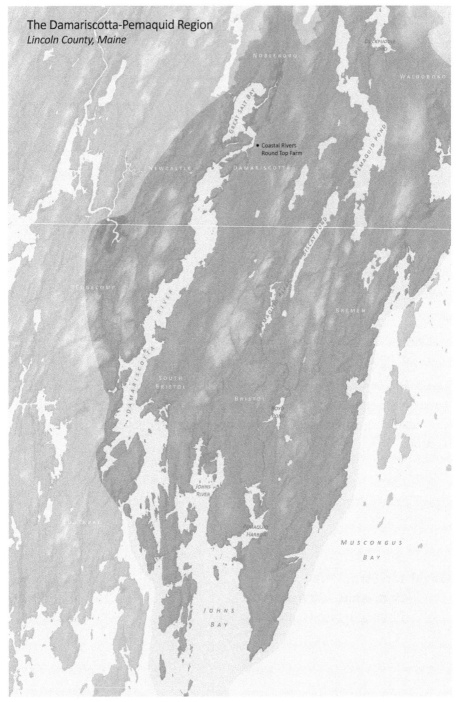

The Damariscotta-Pemaquid Region
Lincoln County, Maine

Photos opposite: (above) the upper river middens
(below) spawning Alewives

Damariscotta River Estuary

The Damariscotta-Pemaquid region is defined by its waterways. The richly productive Damariscotta River Estuary is home to thriving populations of fish, shellfish, waterbirds, and human communities. "Damariscotta" is the corruption of an indigenous name translated as "place of many alewives."[1] Humans have gathered here for millennia to harvest the River's bounty, as evidenced by the ancient shell heaps that may once have held tens of million cubic feet of shells.

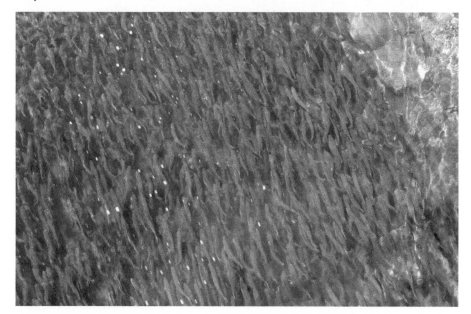

---

[1] Hardy, K. (2009) *Notes on a Lost Flute: A Field Guide to the Wabanaki*. DownEast Books.

Pemaquid River

The Pemaquid River is a serene inland waterway winding nineteen miles down the center of the Pemaquid peninsula, from Tobias Pond in Nobleboro to Pemaquid Mill in Bristol, where it becomes a tidal estuary flowing into Johns Bay. In four stretches along the way, the river expands so broadly and has such narrow inlets and outlets that these areas are more like ponds: Duckpuddle Pond, Pemaquid Pond, Biscay Pond, and Boyd Pond look and behave like ponds, even though they are just wide passages of the Pemaquid River.

Photo: Pemaquid River

(Previous spread) Map Data sources:
USGS Seamless server: NED (1/3 arc sec), NHD, NLCD (30m), .
Maine Office of GIS: Coastline, town boundaries.
Designed by Rhumbline Maps and Coastal Rivers Conservation Trust
All data projected in: UTM 19N, North American Datum 1983.

Johns River

Tucked between South Bristol and Bristol is Johns River. A sparsely developed estuary lined with productive salt marsh and protective forest, Johns River is a nursery ground for fish and other marine creatures, which in turn draw seals and seabirds such as heron, eagles, cormorants, terns, gulls, and osprey.

Photo: Johns River

Coastal Rivers Conservation Trust

To care for these bountiful resources and thriving coastal communities, Coastal Rivers Conservation Trust is charged with protecting water quality, conserving land, providing trails and public access, connecting people to the outdoors through nature education programs, and taking action to confront climate change – both on an organizational level and within the communities we serve.

Coastal Rivers is a non-profit, member-supported, nationally accredited land trust based in Damariscotta, Maine. Learn more at coastalrivers.org.

Round Top Farm

Here, on this land with its rolling hills, mossy forests and waters that run into the Gulf of Maine, we see the cycle of life and remember that this story has repeated itself over and over again. We are grateful and honored to learn from the story that unfolds in this place.

We acknowledge that this is the ancestral and unceded land of the Wabanaki people, including the Pɑnawɑ́hpskewi, Peskotomuhkat, Mi'kmaq and Wolastoqiyik (Passamaquoddy, Penobscot, Micmac and Maliseet).

Since time immemorial, the indigenous ancestors stewarded this land and these waters. At the time of early colonial contact, the Wali ˈnaˈkiak (Wawenock, or people of the bay country) band of the Penobscot tribe lived throughout this region. This place provided everything they needed, and still does.

Photos: (opposite) Round Top Farm barn and fields
              (below) Round Top Trail

For about fifty years, between the early 1920's and the late 1960's, Round Top Farm was a regionally significant dairy farm on the shores of the Upper Damariscotta River and Great Salt Bay. Owned by George and Nancy Freeman, the farm was a large producer of milk and milk products, including the locally famous Round Top Ice Cream (which is still manufactured and sold next door).

Damariscotta River Association inherited the property in 2007 and completed renovation of the old farmhouse in 2019, the same year the organization unified with Pemaquid Watershed Association to form Coastal Rivers Conservation Trust. Today, Coastal Rivers is headquartered here and maintains about a mile and a half of trails through its rolling hayfields, including the accessible Rhoda and Lee Cohen River Trail.

Round Top Farm is open to the public year-round as a place to walk and have picnics, a destination for school field trips, a resource for the community, and the site of the Damariscotta Farmers' Market and Twin Villages Foodbank Farm's Community Food Storage Hub.

THE MEADOW
by AD

THE MEADOW, SHORN DOWN TO THICKEST FUR, LEANING INTO THE RIVER. ON A WALK. I FELT THE SANCTUARY, HOT AND ATOMIC. LOST IN IT. HER TALL TREES ARCHED THEIR BACKS. WE WRAPPED OUR HANDS IN THE FUTURE SOIL. IN MY CAULDRON, I KEPT SOME BLOSSOMS, HERBS, BRIGHT POISON BERRIES. I HAVE SEEN THIS MEADOW FROM ABOVE AND BELOW, THEN PARALLEL. EYES TO EYES TO EYES. FROM OUR RIVER BOATS, FROM THE HARD FLAT ROADS. A MEADOW PULSES AMNIOTIC, HYPNOTIC. THE EXTRATERRESTRIAL SUBMARINE GREENS. AN ORGANISM, THEN DEATH. I WAS AMOEBIC AGAIN. WEIGHT OF HOURS, WEIGHT OF A WATER BODY. WE DID NOT BRING A CAMERA ON THE WALK. I CIRCUMAMBULATED THE MEADOW, CAROUSEL-RIDER, INSECT, DUST, HERRING IN A WHIRLPOOL. IN VISIONS, HERE WE BURIED HORNS, DUG UP ROOTS, SANK OUR NIGHTMARES, RAISED UP CRABS, CLAMS, EARTHWORMS. I WRITHED AGAINST THE STORM OVERHEAD, AND WITH IT. ON A WALK, FIRST DATE. ON A WALK, DATELESS, A DECOMPOSITION. A DISSOLUTION. WHICH MOON WERE WE? WHICH SUN? WOLF MOON, HUNTER'S MOON, SNOW MOON. A PULSE. THE HORSE SHOE CRABS HAD COME AND GONE. ALREADY THE RIVER BANKS LOOKED GREY, THEIR LUSTER LINING THICKENING. I UNBINDED. A COLLAPSE. HERE ICE CREAM GIVES IN TO THE HEAT. SWATTING TICKS, MOSQUITOS, HORSEFLIES. SHADOW OF CROW, SHADOW OF SEAGULL. HOLLERING. THE MILKWEEDS, SWEET AND FIBROUS. THE SCRAPE OF BARK AGAINST SKIN. O! HOW LUSH, ALL OUR INSIDES IN WINTER, THESE UNDERNEATHS. TWO SLUGS SLIPPING ONWARDS. THE DOG SITS DEEP IN THE MUD, REEKS SWEET AND DARK AS POND, WREAKS SYMBIOTIC HAVOC. EXULTATIONS, AN EXHALATION. ON THE ICE, THE SLUSH, THE THAW. TO SEASON IS A VERB. SEASONS, SEASONING. TONGUE INTO MEADOW PULSE. THE DANDELIONS, THEN GRANITE. MICA, CELESTIAL. THE STORM APPROACHES AGAIN, RECEDES. ACROSS THE RIVER, A FOREST. IN THE PARKING LOT, A

PICK-UP TRUCK, REVERSING. SMELL OF STAMEN, DETRITUS, BLOODLESS HANDS. ALL THAT GOES TO SEED. THAT PULSE. THIS PULSE. WE WEAVE WITH WELCOME WEEDS, AND A SWELL, RUSH OF TINY WINGS, TIDES. WE WORK OUR FIGURE EIGHTS, UP AND DOWN THE SLOPES. ON A WALK. AND ANOTHER. DEPARTURE, THEN RETURN. PACING, AGAIN, PACE OF TIDES. THREE CROWS. SEAGULLS. MIRRORS, AMPHIBIOUS LIGHT. KALEIDOSCOPIC, AND SO BRIGHT. WE WALK, LOST IN IT, ALL TORRENTIAL, THEN DRY. FROM OUR RIVER BOATS, LAND-LONGING. FROM LAND, WATER-LONGING. NO ONE WITHOUT THE OTHER. HERE I SHARE SO MANY THINGS, LIKE SECRETS, PLEASANTRIES, FIGHTS. WE DREAM TO BEAR OUR TEETH, LOW, IN THE APPLES, HAUNCHES RUSTLING THE UNDERBRUSH. BEAR OUR TEETH JUST TO LOOK AT THEM. ON A WALK. AGAIN, A CERTAIN LUSTER. ON A WALK ALONE. IN COMPANY. IN THE MEADOW. FEELS LIKE CARE, LIKE SIGHS, LIKE PHOTOSYNTHESES. FIELD OF VISION. VISIONS OF EVERYTHING BENEATH. A CURLING UP, A CLOSENESS. AN OSPREY, ITS CHOREOGRAPHY. HERE THE CENTER, PITS OF OUR ARMS, PITS IN THE STONE, DEEP PITS WHERE THE FRUIT TREES THRUST THEIR PARTS. SEASONS, SEASONING. A LOW RUMBLE. AN ACHE. A RUSH. SALTS. HUNGER. NO I DON'T WANT TO KNOW WHAT IT IS, I WANT TO KNOW WHAT HAPPENS IN A PLACE LIKE THIS. ON A WALK. AGAIN. I FELT THE MEADOW PULSE.

AN EXHALATION
by AD

THE BARN, WORN-IN GRASSES.
THE TREES LOOKED BLACK AND WET
BURSTS OF GREEN, ABOVE AND BELOW,
BLUE IRIDESCENCE, SOLAR PANELS, AND NIGHTTIMES
I HEARD THE RIVER
MOON POWERED, MUSCULAR
WHAT'S THE RUSH?
AN EXHALATION. I FELT ALL
THE FARM'S TENDERNESSES.
THE FEEDING AND THE WATERING. I THOUGHT
ABOUT FEASTS AND FASTING, AND JUST HOW FAST
IT WAS ALL HAPPENING — BRIGHT-BACKED INSECTS,
THEIR PREPARATIONS. CASUAL, OPERATIC.
THE RIVER WAS LOUD,
THEN LOUDER STILL. I WALKED UP THE HILLS,
THEN DOWN, ALL THE PUDDLES, DEEPER THAN
THEY LOOKED.
ROSE HIPS, PINES, SOME KIND OF ASH —
AND JUST HOW SLOW.

THE NATURE CONSERVANCY

Missouri

To conserve the lands and waters on which all life depends.

That simple statement creates the framework for what we do. It helps us determine our priorities and figure out when to say yes and when to say no. It keeps us aimed in the right direction when a thousand distractions threaten to pull us off course.

All of that is important, critical even. But it is not enough to simply *have* a mission in Missouri—we have to be *on* a mission. That difference adds velocity to our work.

TNC's role is unique. We are designed to be a catalyst for conservation. We are a global organization with local agility. Thanks to private funding, we can take risks on innovative techniques that provide the data and test cases that others can then use to drive progress far beyond our own work.

We are conveners. We leverage our resources, science, expertise and networks to facilitate collaboration and build consensus among diverse stakeholders. It's a role that is essential for the kind of large-scale transformative projects that are needed to move the needle.

We look for spaces where we can provide the missing piece for success. But for TNC, these victories wouldn't happen. That's what makes us different.

-Dunn Ranch Prairie
  -Poet and Photographer: Ryan Kegley

The Nature Conservancy—Missouri

Organization Overview

Founded in the U.S. through grassroots action in 1951, The Nature Conservancy has grown to become one of the most effective and wide-reaching environmental organizations in the world. We partner with communities across the globe to overcome the barriers to climate and biodiversity solutions.

Thanks to more than a million members and the dedicated efforts of our diverse staff and over 400 scientists, we impact conservation in 79 countries and territories: 37 by direct conservation impact and 42 through partners.

A World Where People and Nature Thrive

We believe that a world where people and nature thrive is possible. And although that world may feel far away right now, we know that together, we can find a way there. We know that because, alongside partners, we've spent the past 70 years beating the odds.

As we face the climate and biodiversity crises, the odds seem greater than ever. But working together, we're moving forward. We succeed by reaching beyond boundaries and borders, across common grounds and great divides. We rely on cutting-edge science and age-old wisdom. And we guide game-changing decisions and forge new funding. No matter the odds, together we find the people and the paths to make change possible.

The Nature Conservancy in Missouri

Just five years after TNC's inception, the Conservancy opened a chapter in Missouri. Since 1956, we've been working to protect and steward our land and water resources in the state.

When we look across Missouri today, we see the progress of decades of work as well as continued need and possibilities: ranchers hoping to preserve a way of life for the next generation, Ozark streams that are the last refuge for species that live nowhere else and school kids ready to expand their world.

We move forward by building trust, demonstrating solutions, inspiring change and collaborating with the communities, agencies and decision-makers who can adopt more sustainable practices and make change. Our task has been to eliminate the barriers that stand in the way. Fortunately, finding innovative solutions is what we do best. That means digging in, literally, to rebuild riverbanks that protect drinking water for small towns and habitat for vulnerable wildlife. It means providing lawmakers the science-based information they need to make the best decisions. It means ensuring everyone has access to benefits and nature.

We know the risks of doing nothing. The effects of a changing climate and rapidly declining biodiversity are already altering Missouri in ways that affect the health, economy and well-being of the state. But we also know that nature is resilient and that Missourians are working every day toward solutions.

Solutions to Protect Our Lands

Missouri packs a world of landscapes into one state. Deep-rooted prairies, adorned with hundreds of species of grasses and wildflowers. Caves that number in the thousands. Ancient Ozark mountains that predate the Rockies by more than a billion years.

More than 100 natural communities, with unique terrain and inhabitants, live within Missouri's borders. This variety is embedded in the state's marrow, but it will take a dogged effort, rooted in science, to carry it into the future.

The Nature Conservancy took up the mission to conserve and protect Missouri's vital landscapes more than 60 years ago. We work to boost biodiversity, repairing and nurturing the habitats that shelter native plants and wildlife. That has long included stewarding our preserves across the state, but the mission extends beyond property lines. With the help of our partners, we leverage our preserves to develop, test and demonstrate practices that are good for the land and that make good financial sense for landowners and communities.

We share those lessons and pitch in to support conservation efforts across the state. More than 93 percent of Missouri land is privately owned. For people and nature to thrive, it will take all of us working together.

Whether it's helping ranchers implement sustainable grazing methods or teaming up with state fire crews on ecosystem-restoring prescribed fires, conservation-minded land management practices have a powerful impact. They can boost soil fertility, sequester carbon, conserve water and create habitat. Working with others to create solutions and put those solutions to work is crucial to building a strong, healthy Missouri.

Dunn Ranch Prairie

Dunn Ranch Prairie is a nearly 4,000-acre tallgrass preserve in northwest Missouri. Once just a drop in the sea of grasslands that covered a third of the United States, the land within its boundaries is now a rare holdover of that iconic landscape. The majority of North America's grasslands were plowed under, built over or otherwise destroyed by the mid-20th century. Less than 1 percent remains today.

The Nature Conservancy bought the core of the preserve in 1999 from descendants of the Dunn family. The original 2,281 acres included about 1,000 acres that had never been touched by a plow. Later additions have grown the preserve to its current size.

TNC staff, with the help of partners and dedicated volunteers, have worked to restore the prairie, collecting native seeds, often by hand, for grasses and forbs. Bluestem, switchgrass, coneflowers and hundreds of other species spring forward and recede with the seasons. The ever-changing palette offers habitat to an array of wildlife, such the monarchs that migrate between Mexico and Canada. Prairie-chickens perform their colorful "booming" each spring, upland sandpipers' ghostly calls carry in the wind and river otters glide through grassland streams.

In 2011, TNC reintroduced bison at the preserve. Bison slaughter, driven in part by efforts of the U.S. government to starve Indigenous peoples and force them from their lands, nearly wiped out the species in the late 1800s. The herd in Missouri began with 36 bison from Wind Cave National Park in South Dakota. Now numbering as many as 200, TNC's Missouri herd is key to managing the prairie and supporting the ecosystem. They roll or "wallow" on the ground, making depressions that collect water, and their choosy eating habits give their grazing grounds a patchiness that aids biodiversity.

The bison are a connection to the prairie's past and instrumental in its future. Scientists and school children alike visit Dunn Ranch Prairie every year to learn about the bison and the grasslands. The herd is now healthy enough that there are excess bison each season. In partnership with Native peoples-led partnerships, bison from TNC herds, including those at Dunn, are routinely transferred to Tribal lands so that they can help renew relationships and build a future for prairies and people.

The Hunter
by Ryan Kegley

You announced your arrival with a raspy squawk
and alighted at the edge of the pond. The sun
was setting, and the air, buoyant for July,
was livelier still with the conversations and carrying-ons
of common yellowthroat, dickcissel, barn and cliff
swallow, American robin, upland sandpiper,
house and song sparrow, all dancing atop
the sonorous bellow of solicitous bullfrogs. You,
more Jurassic than modern, a gangly but graceful
serpent on stilts, noticed neither them nor me
as you stalked your prey. I've never seen such patience.
A step. A pause. A tilt of the head. Another step,
more studied than the last. Stealthily you made
your way across the water, each footfall soundless,
rippleless. Twenty minutes to traverse twenty feet.
A step, a pause, a crane of the neck, the crouch.
The interminable wait. Then at last the strike,
so swift and surgical that had I blinked I would
have missed it. Spellbound, I watched once more
before the sun passed beyond the hills, and you
disappeared behind a stand of grasses. I thought,
I should like to be like you, *Ardea herodias,* treading
lightly, leaving no wake, infinitely patient, my days
as deliberate as each glacial stride made in that pond.

Defiance
by Ryan Kegley

for Dunn Ranch Prairie

What happens here is not the stuff of cutting-
edge technologies, of machine learning, of artificial
intelligence, of augmented humans and augmented
analytics and augmented design, of intelligent
spaces and smart places, of blockchains, of natural
language processing, of cloud and edge and quantum
computing, of big data, of machine co-creativity,
of computer vision and facial recognition, of digital
twins and digital platforms and digitally extended
realities, of gene editing, of drones, of chatbots
and robots and cobots, of cybersecurity and cyber
resilience, of micro-moments and mass personalization,
of 4D printing, additive manufacturing, the new
space race or the Internet of Things, but a simple act
of defiance: stewarding the present into the future
by honoring the past.

In Which We May Be Reborn
by Ryan Kegley

Daybreak, lately punctuated with cumulonimbus
only Davis could paint, has turned to Richter's panes
of monochrome gray. Rain is in the air, pregnant
and cool and damp, more spring than high summer.
In this living landscape of virgin prairie, in the midst
of American buffalo, *Bison bison bison*, returned
to their sacred calling, I am witness to deep time.

I see the wild plains, unfenced and unfettered, grasses
stretching as far as the eye can see, bison teeming
in their thousands, in their tens of thousands
and with them the Báxoje, traditional caretakers
of these ancestral lands. Eyes closed, I hear Dodge's call,
Kill every buffalo you can! Every buffalo dead is
an Indian gone. I sat in the utterness of those words,

the soft grass of my heart weeping for what might
have been. At last, thunder rolls thick and strong,
winds snapping to attention, the sturdy rains washing
over the land, over bird and butterfly and milkweed,
over deer and coyote and bison, over the forgotten,
over the fallen and the dispossessed, over the sins of our
grandfathers' grandfathers' grandfathers.

Oxytocin
by Ryan Kegley

You are not in the middle of nowhere. Here, in the Grand
River Grasslands of northern Missouri, the landscape looks

like so much drive-by land—something full of nothing
on your way to somewhere else. Stay awhile. If you're

unaccustomed, the first minute can be uncomfortable.
Relax. Find a spot on the ground. Sit. Five minutes

can feel formidable. Where is my phone? Am I missing
out? Does someone need me? Breathe. Feel the air fill

your lungs, deeper and more fully than you've ever felt.
Feel the release that comes in the exhale. Let go. Surrender

your impulse to action. After ten minutes, a clarity takes
hold, the clutter and clatter of the everyday evaporating

like valley fog on a summer morning. There is nothing
but you, outside your body, beyond the self, in this place,

this nowhere, this everywhere, this prairie that is emptiness
and fullness altogether. Synthesis and antithesis.

After thirty minutes, you can't imagine going back:
Indiangrass and bluestem rustling in the breeze, the damp

patter of rain from an incoming storm, the immediate
and all-encompassing drone of cicadas and with it the chirps

of cricket and trills of katydid, and the birds, first crow,
biggest and loudest, followed by bellicose jay, then bunting,

too, with his lively song of what! what! where? where?
see it! see it! and whip-poor-will's namesake refrain,

emphatic and endless, the dazzling colors of blazing star,
gentian, aster and sunflower, lake upon sea upon ocean

of sunflower, the panoramic grandeur of bison browsing
before you, the rich smell of humus, mystical and physiological,

human and humane, from and of the earth, bonds lover
to loved, child to mother, you to mother earth: Your once-

coarse senses awakened and alive to the once-foreign world
around you. Stay as long as you can. Hold that other

world at bay, if only a little longer. When you go, carry this
moment with you, this time spent here in this somewhere,

in this place that is no longer nowhere. Hold it, real
and vital and necessary, as you hold love, as you hold truth,

as you hold all the days of your life.

FORTERRA

Washington

FORT&RRA
LAND FOR GOOD

Forterra innovates and scales land-based solutions to address the climate crisis and support equitable, green and prosperous communities.

Forterra envisions people and nature thriving together in a place where everyone belongs.

-Camp Kilworth
        -Poet: Susan Landgraf
        -Photos by Forterra
-Hazel Wolf Wetlands Preserve
        -Poet: Jill McCabe Johnson
        -Photographer: Todd Parker

Forterra

Forterra is Washington state's largest non-profit land trust working across Washington state's diverse communities and landscapes. We proudly consider ourselves an unconventional land trust in what we do, how we do it and with whom.

In our first 35 years, Forterra has conserved more than 275,000 acres of geographically diverse lands and places at risk. Wild lands and working lands in both urban and rural settings. Our efforts span the estuaries, farms, and forests of Washington's coast, and reach the ranches and shrub-steppe of the Yakima basin.

Forterra recognizes that how we do our work is as important as what we seek to achieve. We bring people together for landscape-scale approaches that address climate change, population growth, and social equity. We recognize the different connectivity of the landscapes, and the different ways we live, work, and play there.

Our success is grounded in convening likely and unlikely partners for collective land-centered solutions. Innovative and holistic approaches that connect community and conservation – people and place.

It's a strategy we call *land for good*. And it's about providing for the full needs of our ecosystem and society. From protecting treasured environmental spaces to supporting livable cities and towns with community-informed development and affordable housing.

That's Forterra's vision – people and nature thriving together in a place where everyone belongs.

Land for good is indeed land for all.

Camp Kilworth

Home to one of our region's few youth camps, and providing critical salmon-rearing habitat, Camp Kilworth in Federal Way (south of Seattle) closed in 2016 and was nearly lost for good to development. Forterra recognized the immeasurable cost of losing this 80-year-old lifeline to the natural world.

When locals formed the Kilworth Environmental Education Preserve to make their voices heard, Forterra listened. We purchased the property in 2022 to fulfill the community's goals and worked to create a partnership with the YMCA of Greater Seattle, granting a 50-year lease to provide youth programming for the region. Together, we are restoring Camp Kilworth to promote the health and well-being of youth once again with environmental education accessible for everyone. The camp was slated to re-open in summer 2024 for kids, the community and for special emphasis on Tribal use. Beyond outdoor programs developed by the YMCA, the Puyallup Tribe will provide Indigenous outdoor education programs for campers. The Tribe also will receive site access for cultural purposes.

"The Puyallup people have been stewards of these lands since time immemorial, and this property has special historical and cultural significance. Partnerships with entities like Forterra help the Tribe actively conserve natural and cultural resources in areas facing major development pressures," said the Puyallup Tribal Council.

Camp Kilworth conserves one of the area's last undeveloped shorelines with nearly 30 acres of high-bank forest and a corridor for bald eagles and herons. Forterra is pleased to conserve this site in perpetuity.

History of Sounds in the South Sound of the Salish Sea
by Susan Landgraf

First
the sound of wind over the ice
over
the hot belly of the Great Mother.

Then wind and the ice breaking, mountains rising,
Mt. Tahoma belching into being.
The birth of red.

Wind and the sound of rivers
flowed over the Great Mother's children –
stones and salmon birthed upstream
swimming to the sea, then back to spawn and die.

Sunrises, sunsets and wind shared the sky
with red cedars, hemlock, pines, later alders,
big leaf maples and madrones, with ravens,
red-breasted sapsuckers, great horned owls
and cliff swallows.

The Puyallup harvested red huckleberry,
salmonberry, nettles. They smoked salmon,
crafted cedar canoes; their oars sliced
the waves, sounds of their drums and chants
keeping time –

followed by saws, falling trees, hammers hitting nails,
tires hissing on highways –

except
in this place
on the lip of a cliff with second-growth trees
a camp for children
where they can listen to the wilderness in the middle
of a city – flute-like call of a Swainson's thrush,

a coyote's howl, and cedar roots
talking underground

in this place
filled in the winter
when the wind occasionally sleeps
with the sound of silence.

Winter at Camp Kilworth, December 2023
by Susan Landgraf

Fog wraps
the green sentinels
in silence

As always the trees
are in conversation
with the firs and ferns

human footprints
buried in the duff of leaves
and skeletons

invasive ivy
and old buildings gone
debris and trails cleared

In the fog, green
sentinels wait for next
summer, for children

The children will come
to learn what a night is
without lights

sleep on the cliff
above the sea with the land
under their backs

listen to an owl
and rain falling through
a leafed canopy

Some children will
translate what the First People
and green sentinels

salmon, eelgrass beds
and bats have all been saying
Save us.

Hazel Wolf Wetlands Preserve

The Pacific Northwest's conservation community has long been invigorated by the tenacity and foresight of activist and environmentalist Hazel Wolf. A self-described rabble rouser, Hazel's spirit lives on at the Hazel Wolf Wetlands Preserve – one of the most pristine wetland-based wildlife refuges in King County. These biologically rich 116 acres were preserved in 1995 through an innovative partnership.

Neighbors, led by Ann and Fred Weinmann, recognized these as some of the highest-quality wetlands on the Sammamish Plateau. They worked with landowners, King County government, and corporate partners to protect this natural area sought after by developers in a rapidly urbanizing landscape.

Forterra joined the partnership to craft a precedent-setting agreement that continues to serve as a preservation agreement model today. The Hazel Wolf Wetlands Preserve is a prized gem in Forterra's land portfolio. It's open to the public, offering trails that lace through rich vegetation with diverse species. It also connects to the extensive trails network that runs through Beaver Lake Preserve and Soaring Eagle Regional Park.

Walking the Hazel Wolf Loop
by Jill McCabe Johnson

Late afternoon threads through Western hemlock
         as we walk this wetland trail. In spring
we search for trillium blossoms and chocolate lily.

In summer foxglove spires in open spaces.
         Today we delve deep into autumn's lure.
We promised to leave our worries at the trailhead,

         your sister's diagnosis,
my brother's car accident,
         the latest declarations of war.

For now, we are co-travelers winding through ironwood,
         snowberry, and coast grand fir. You admire
a waterfall of ferns wisping down a craggy trunk.

         I'm entranced by small villages of mushrooms
sprouting in the underbrush. Little brown creepers
         skip along willow branches and a pair

of Canadian snow geese ripples sunlight off the water.
         You stop and reach for my hand
as the birds drift in and out of view.

Reading the Woods
by Jill McCabe Johnson

Red-breasted sapsuckers tattooed holes
in horizontal lines on tender paper birch.
The markings match scar-like lentices
raked over trunk and limb.

After rain, low-hanging willow branches
seem to swim in their own reflection
where runoff streams over grasses
that sway in the current too.

A downed alder floats among the reeds,
its trunk speckled with the neon-orange
of jelly spot fungus fruiting from within
the wet and nourishing wood.

A row of western redcedar saplings
casts feathery shadows over the nurselog
where their long root tendrils
burrow for foothold and food.

Here, you don't have to see the branches
to know this mulch of tiny cones
belongs to lacy western hemlock
whose needles murmur in the breeze.

And was it the North American beaver or small
mountain beaver who gnawed the shorn maples?
Their confetti of wood shavings
dots layers of fallen leaves.

Becoming Merganser
by Jill McCabe Johnson

What if you could fold your wings
          and glide on silky waters?

When friends visit, you'll bob your head
          up and down and shiver with excitement.

Maybe you can join their flotilla of feathers
          parading in a line near shore.

Imagine getting hungry and diving beak-first
          to fish in your underwater buffet.

Later, you can nap in the reeds,
          serenaded by tree frogs singing out their love.

Don't worry. If a raptor appears, Northern Flicker's
          shrill warning will wake you.

For dinner you can stomp in a mud puddle
          to charm the earthworms and grubs.

Come night you will nest in the hollow of a cedar snag,
          a fluff of ducklings cozied beneath your wing.

BLUE HILL HERITAGE TRUST

COMMUNITY BASED LAND CONSERVATION SINCE 1985

**BLUE HILL
HERITAGE TRUST**

Maine

Blue Hill Heritage Trust's Mission:

- To lead in conserving land, water, and wildlife habitat on the greater Blue Hill Peninsula.

- To teach and practice a stewardship ethic.

- To promote ecological, economic, and community health for this and future generations.

-The Penobscot Community Forest at Wallamatogus Mountain
  -Poet: Stuart Kestenbaum
  -Photographer: Chrissy Allen

Blue Hill Heritage Trust

Blue Hill Heritage Trust is a community based conservation organization on the Blue Hill Peninsula along the Downeast coast of Maine. Our peninsula sits between Penobscot Bay and Blue Hill Bay and is just west of Acadia National Park. This is the traditional territory of the Wabanaki, specifically Penobscot and Passamaquoddy peoples. Today this coast is best known for recreation and the lobster fishery, but the peninsula had a robust nineteenth-century economy in mining and quarrying. Granite particularly was sent from the Blue Hill Peninsula all over the United States and the world during that period.

Through our 38-year history, BHHT has become increasingly sophisticated in our conservation work. We conserve land, water, and wildlife habitat on our peninsula, we teach and practice a stewardship ethic on our lands, and we promote ecological, economic, and community health. We think of conservation as both enhancing the land's ability for self-renewal and engaging people with the land which supports our communities and economies. We have protected over 12,000 acres, since our founding in 1985, and we now steward that land for future generations. We judge land projects through science-based criteria, in this era of climate change, and approach conservation as a community endeavor.

BHHT has undergone intellectual development alongside organizational growth, and we have been a leader in the conservation community. We were early practitioners of farmland conservation in Maine, using mechanisms like "buy-restrict-sell" to protect farmland and lower the entry price for new farmers. We continue our commitment to farmland and farmers, and this is part of our larger philosophy of protecting and stewarding working landscapes for community benefit.

In the past, BHHT developed a broad network of trails across the peninsula, creating community benefit through recreational access. More recently, we have focused on age-friendly, accessible trails to be more inclusive in meeting needs. Maintaining these trails is a considerable part of BHHT stewardship, in both financing and capacity.

Engaging community through expanded public access remains central to our work, as do our growing educational programs. These began as a wide variety of offerings focused on BHHT land, and have become increasingly focused on land stewardship, outdoor education for school kids, and creating mutually beneficial relationships between people and our woodlands and wild places.

Our vision is to carry forward our history of expanding this philosophy of conservation and community. Both in the evolution of public engagement and the evolution of public attitudes about BHHT, it is increasingly clear that our work has grown from being an added benefit to life here on the Blue Hill Peninsula into something more vital. We expect further development in our expanding role in the community.

Blue Hill Heritage Trust acknowledges that the land we conserve is part of the homeland of Wabanaki peoples who have lived in this region from time immemorial, and who remain sovereign tribal nations – distinct legal and political entities with the powers of self-governance and self-determination.

BHHT expresses our deepest respect for and gratitude to these original and ongoing stewards of the land, recognizing the historical and ongoing harm to their culturally important and sacred places. As an organization, we acknowledge our responsibility to establish and maintain relationships with Wabanaki peoples, and to include their voices and concerns in our conservation work. To those ends, we begin our understanding of conserved land with their long history and continued connection to this peninsula, a legacy from which we all benefit.

The Penobscot Community Forest on Wallamatogus Mountain

The Penobscot Community Forest on Wallamatogus Mountain is 336 acres of both woodland and open blueberry barrens. It was the site of the Leech homestead in the nineteenth century and was a commercial blueberry field from the 1950s to 2016. The top of the mountain offers one of the best views on the Blue Hill Peninsula, overlooking Penobscot Bay, the Bagaduce River watershed, and Acadia National Park in the distance.

The land was conserved in 2021 with the help of many partners including The Conservation Fund, Land for Maine's Future, and US Forest Service Community Forest Grant program. The town of Penobscot facilitated access across town property for parking and part of the trail to the summit.

From the trailhead, the path leads through the woods and then across the wide-open field as it heads toward the summit. In many ways, the view standing in the lower part of the field is as dramatic as the view from the top, looking across the open expanse toward the top. For many years, this has been a spot treasured by locals, and it is now open to the public.

Photo (above): Blueberries on Wallamatogus Mountain
Photo (previous spread): Southern slope of Wallamatogus Mountain
overlooking Penobscot Bay

Elegy
by Stuart Kestenbaum

Wallamatogus Mountain
Penobscot, Maine

We are always measuring time,
like the way we mark our children's
heights on the door jamb, the way
in the old movies the calendar pages
fly off into space as the years pass.
Here it is measured in the white pines
and birches making their way into
the blueberry field, the goldenrod
and pearly everlasting waving
in early September's warm breeze,
the air hazy from forest fires
thousands of miles distant in Canada.
This morning I am the only human on the mountain,
except for the family at rest in the overgrown
burial plot under the tall maple.
The lichen have been at work on the rough
and polished surfaces of the headstones,
the same way they began their patient
work on the boulders left when the glaciers receded.
Ella L. wife of Elisha Leach,
Died Aug 30, 1901
50 yrs. 4 mos. 29 dys,
an inscription that keeps track
of one life so specifically that all
that is missing are the hours, minutes, and seconds
of that final day. Imagine that last breath
the one that helps us sing with joy
and makes mourners of us all.

Photo (above): Leach Family Cemetery on Wallamatogus Mountain
Photo (below): Stone structure on Wallamatogus Mountain overlooking
Blue Hill Mountain and Acadia National Park in the distance

Photo (above): GoldenRod and native bees on Wallamatogus Mountain
Photo (below): Doggy enjoying the views from Wallamatogus Mountain

Summer's End
by Stuart Kestenbaum

A few months before the blueberry fields
turn crimson, a few days after the Blue Hill Fair,

where the Ferris wheel
lifts us above the screams

of the bumper cars and Gravitron
eleven thousand years since the glaciers receded

and left the landscape strewn with boulders
I walk through the blueberry field

on Wallamatogus Mountain.
Halfway up the slope blue plastic boxes

left behind by the last human harvesters
as if someone had stopped

in the middle of a job and walked away.
Soon the season will become cooler air

and brilliant light reflecting off the water.
Some days I don't know whether

I should weep or sing.
This year's berries are gone by,

but I discover a few near the footpath.
I expected there would be

none left behind,
but here they are on my tongue,

these sweet, dark blue worlds,
orbiting the sun with me.

Photo: Hiking up the old jeep roads on Wallamatogus Mountain

MARIN AGRICULTURAL LAND TRUST

California

Marin Agricultural Land Trust (MALT)'s mission is to permanently protect Marin's agricultural land for agricultural use.

MALT's vision for Marin County is a thriving and inclusive agricultural community in a healthy and diverse natural environment.

-Straus Home Ranch
    -Poet: Heather Bourbeau
    -Photographer: Jeff Lewis

Marin Agricultural Land Trust

In the 1960s, Marin County—across the Golden Gate Bridge from San Francisco—had plans for a massive suburban development project on its coast. Freeways had been mapped and surveyed to cut across the county's farmland and land prices were rising. For the struggling dairy industry, it seemed like the beginning of the end.

But in the coming years, a group of ranchers and citizen activists forged an unlikely alliance that successfully protected the county's agricultural landscape from this suburban sprawl proposal. Through mutual respect and growing trust, a new chapter of land conservation began to take root.

In 1980, Ellen Straus and Phyllis Faber—a local dairywoman and a botanist—furthered this alliance by founding the Marin Agricultural Land Trust (MALT). As the first farmland trust in the nation, MALT trailblazed the purchase of development rights from landowners to protect the land, preserve its agricultural community, and promote local food.

Photo: Straus Home Ranch (166 acres) Overlooking Tomales Bay, Straus Home Ranch supports pasture for dairy replacement heifers. The ranch, once owned by Ellen Straus, one of the founding members of MALT, hosts agro-tourism events in the historic ranch house and barn.

To date, MALT has safeguarded more than 55,000 acres of land—a testament to the community's success, found in an unlikely union to protect an incredible landscape.

For more than forty years, the Marin Agricultural Land Trust (MALT) has invested in the protection and stewardship of both working and natural lands. Today, the organization and its partners celebrates $100 million invested in land conservation and it continues to serve as a beacon of hope—a national example for others in the pursuit of local farmland conservation.

MALT's primary objective is the preservation of agricultural lands. Through conservation easements, MALT collaborates with willing landowners, allowing them to voluntarily restrict their land from non-agricultural development. This innovative approach not only safeguards the rural character of Marin County but also helps to maintain the economic viability of local farms.

Photo: Black Mountain Ranch (1,190 acres) MALT's easement on this ranch protects the west face of Black Mountain, a prominent West Marin landmark. Organic pastures are leased for grazing beef cattle, and the ranch is also home to two small organic farms.

To date, MALT has secured 93 agricultural conservation easements totaling more than 55,700 acres of farm and ranchland—the backbone of Marin County's agricultural economy.

MALT also offers financial assistance and technical expertise for land stewardship efforts. Through its grantmaking programs, MALT bolsters the health of the region's agricultural landscape, strengthening the local economy and securing the natural infrastructure that safeguards nearby communities.

While there's much to celebrate, MALT's work is far from over. Nearly half of Marin County's working landscapes remain without conservation easements and the future of agriculture remains threatened by rising costs, changing weather patterns, housing shortages impacting the agricultural community, and so much more.

To help guide MALT's efforts over the next few years, we have organized our work around five strategic pillars: focusing on preserving agriculture, protecting biodiversity, building climate resilience, connecting community, and strengthening the organization. While these pillars have been fundamental for much of our legacy to date, there's never been a more important time for MALT to thrive and now is the time to double down.

Photo: Millerton Creek Ranch (862 acres) To protect this property, MALT purchased this ranch from a real estate developer, leased it temporarily to two local ranchers, and ultimately sold them the ranch with a conservation easement in place.

Photos: (above) Black Mountain Ranch; (below) Millerton Creek Ranch

Featured Property: Straus Home Ranch (166 acres)

Overlooking Tomales Bay, Straus Home Ranch supports pasture for dairy replacement heifers. The ranch, once owned by Ellen Straus, one of the founding members of MALT, hosts agro-tourism events in the historic ranch house and barn.

Photo: Straus Home Ranch

High Summer
by Heather Bourbeau

In the year of the water rabbit, tall, dry grasses swirl.
Lapping wind, weight of hooves.

Raven and hawk circle and hunt
gopher, deer mouse, shrew-mole, dreams.

The drip of beard lichen from branches,
the burst of yellow bird's-foot trefoil, bristly oxtongue.

I scan my legs for ticks, pick burrs from my socks—
unsubtle, these reminders of explorations, intrusions.

Last week, in Ireland, in light rain, I walked counter-clockwise
around a holy well. I knelt and cupped my right hand,

brought water to my face, my heart,
thanked the river for all it had given.

But we have made our gods fickle and withholding.
To the east are floods, to the north—fires.

For the moment, here, I am safe,
grateful for the fog that burns slowly over Tomales Bay.

In the autumn, elders and school children will gather,
plant and seed native growth to restore the creek bed,

hold the water, soften the scars of men.
Soon, I think, I may walk this line, feel the slick

of mud, relish the quick return of insects,
the slow growth of hope.

Symbiosis
by Heather Bourbeau

Human boundaries distinguished by gate and barb,
wood and rust. Crickets rub legs seemingly silently.
The whistle songs of lesser goldfinches fill the air.
Last week, a fox ate a chicken.
Poor Marcia, dear Marcia.
                    Lucky fox.

As a child I was warned of rattlesnake and bear. Remote Siskiyou cabin.
Coffee pot crushed by an unseen ursus—a caution kept in the kitchen.
The oldest of the cousins were taught to shoot in defense.
The youngest how to act big, stay calm.
I do not remember being scared.
                    Not of bear.

Seeking insects, foraging bears tear apart logs, dig plants and roots
from the ground, assist in decomposition.
They shit berries, acorns, fruits and distribute seeds.
Black bears used to be here, then we hunted them out.
But last year, one was seen across this narrow bay.
                    Scat and scratches on trees.

Now a friend asks me to confirm his suspicions.
Shows me photos of shit, thick and brown, almost cow-like.
I bring out my book. We scan the photos. Like hagiologists
we hope to confirm a minor miracle.
I vacillate between elk and black bear with an acorn diet, thinking
                    It is too early for acorns.

Then I realize, "too early," "too late,"
"too hot," "too dry"—these are all meaningless now.
Nearby, a tree twists around itself, allows another to grow inside.
As the sun sets, in the overgrown bramble,
I reach past thorns to pick ripe blackberries. Juice on tongue,
                    stain on hands.

Photo (above): Black Mountain Ranch
Photo (next page): Spring blooms amid the MALT-protected Leiss Ranch

DHARMAKAYA CENTER FOR WELLBEING

New York

DHARMAKAYA
CENTER FOR WELLBEING

In a natural spiritual setting, the Dharmakaya Center for Wellbeing provides a wide range of practices drawn from ancient wisdom, for all levels of interest, in order to cultivate physical and emotional wellbeing in the greatest number of people. Grounded in Buddhist traditions, the Center sits at the intersection of ancient wisdom and contemporary wellbeing. With a focus on both mind and body, we believe that physical wellbeing creates a positive environment for mental health; mental wellbeing produces a sense of equanimity that is the foundation for physical health. We invite you to join us.

-Poet: Stacey Z. Lawrence

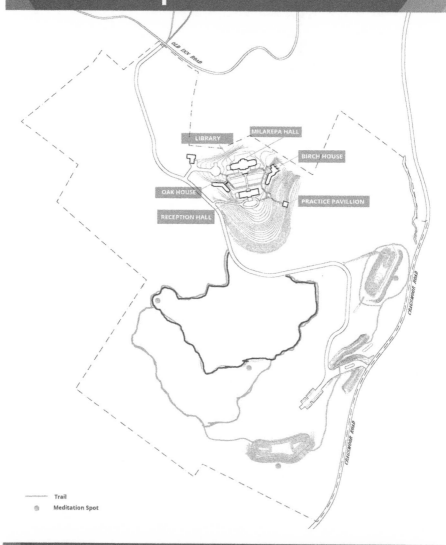

The Dharmakaya Center for Wellbeing

The Dharmakaya Center for Wellbeing sits on 90 acres high in the northern Shawangunk Ridge, outside the hamlet of Cragsmoor, New York. The ridge, formed approximately 250 million years ago, is widely recognized as one of the most important sites for biodiversity conservation in the northeastern United States. The ridge's higher elevations are covered with unique pine-barrens, while the slopes support New York's largest known chestnut oak forest.

In the early 19th century, the land was part of the Decker farm; later it held the Cragsmoor Inn, an outstanding local hotel for more than 30 years. Then the property remained vacant for decades. In 2004, Dharmakaya Inc. bought the land to house a new meditation retreat center. A nine-year planning process led to the groundbreaking ceremony on July 18, 2013; the Center opened in July, 2017.

Trungram Gyalwa Rinpoche, PhD conceived of and founded the Dharmakaya Center in order to share ancient Buddhist teachings in ways that are responsive to a 21st Century way of life. Rinpoche chose the Catskills in support of the people of greater New York following the tragedy of September 11, 2001. After much searching, he selected the property in Cragsmoor because of its inherent spiritual feeling.

People often comment on the sense of peace that envelops them from the moment they pass through the gates. The driveway curves up the mountain, with two ponds flanking the road. Open areas offer sweeping views of wildflower meadows. Trails wend through the surrounding woods. Cairns dot the property; according to Tibetan Buddhist belief, they call in good fortune and balance conflicting energies. The land beckons.

And our guests respond. They find spots to sit in contemplation, on seats carved into fallen trees and benches carved from old logs, meditating on a strategically placed Buddha, a lovely stand of trees or birds darting through the reeds around a pond. They perform kora, a walking meditation clockwise through the woods.

And many engage in forest bathing, immersing themselves in nature, and experiencing it with all five senses. Adherents find themselves in touch with present-moment experience in a very deep way, noticing and sensing things rather than judging or evaluating them. This practice is shown to have profound benefits for physical health, lowering blood pressure and increasing immunity; it also improves mental health.

In all these meditative practices, emotions rise, stir, evaporate as our guests and retreatants settle into deep inner contemplation—learning to harness the skills of awareness.

ashes
by Stacey Z Lawrence

near a cackling
pot belly flame
the silvery man-in-charge
drops
small explosions
of starch & sap
splashes of marshmallow
across dark graveled mugs
as children unwrap
beneath dappled
patterns of light,
crumpled xmas paper
all higgledy-piggledy
amid kin
they ring
around the rosey
& all fall
down.

Pastoral Symphony
by Stacey Z Lawrence

—*For Larry*

I sit silent & still
atop a catskill knoll beyond
cacophony & squawk squawk, squawk
sucking raw to the bone I listen through
lightning   slicing
those songs, those god-Damn
          songs, you funneled
          down our little street
          they were Beethoven

& I think that is what I meant to say
that day
          after you died
when we placed stones
on small motes
under sun that
hung above us
like a huge black disc
like the gloomiest record in your collection
we studied them all
which is how I kissed the tang of poetry
through rock operas & bohemian rhapsodies
sleeves in ripe verse strewn across the carpet

& I imagine you now with
Tommy Walker & Ziggy Stardust
the three of you
lounging on a pew
inhaling in the Houses of the Holy
thundering music together
like nobody is listening.

meditations
by Stacey Z Lawrence

the sphere
of your smile
the trapezoid
of your desk
the cylinder
of your smoke
the triangle
of our tent
the cone
of our blunt
the heart
of our love
the star
of our young
the rectangle
of your glass
the column
of your skis
the hemisphere
of your mind
the oval
of our tears
the decagon
of lamotrigine
the octagon
of doxepin
the square patch
of fentanyl
the hexagon
of clonazepam
the heptagon
of lorazepam
the spiral
of IV drip drip drip
the funnel

of carboplatin
the prism
of the dropper
the parallelogram
of the sheet
the rectangle
of the bag
the crescent
of the moon
the cross
of the church.
the line,
mine.

Poets' Biographies

Jan Bindas-Tenney is a white trans non-binary & queer writer, reader, fighter, lover, friend and parent living on unceded Abenaki land now called South Portland, Maine. They hold an MFA in non-fiction from University of Arizona. Their writing has appeared in *Orion, Guernica, Gulf Coast, Arts & Letters, CutBank, the Maine Review,* among other places. They work at the Vera Institute of Justice. They live and love with their partner Rachael, kids Sonny, Avi & dog Bisbee.

Heather Bourbeau's work has appeared in *Alaska Quarterly Review, The Kenyon Review, Meridian, The Stockholm Review of Literature,* and *SWWIM.* She has worked with various UN agencies, including the UN peacekeeping mission in Liberia and UNICEF Somalia. Her collection *Some Days The Bird* is a poetry conversation with poet Anne Casey (Beltway Editions, 2022). Her latest collection *Monarch* explores overlooked histories from the US West (Cornerstone Press, 2023).

Mike Bove is the author of four books, most recently *EYE* (Spuyten Duyvil, 2023). He was winner of the 2021 Maine Postmark Poetry Contest and a 2023 finalist for a Maine Literary Award. He is Professor of English at Southern Maine Community College and lives with his family in Portland, Maine where he was born and raised. mikebove.com

AD / Anna M. Drzewiecki is an artist, writer, witch, sea farmer, caretaker, and interdisciplinary feminist researcher from Maine. They currently live and study with their dog/familiar, Sauvage, in Oxford, England.

Su Flatt is a Columbus, OH based poet and English professor at Columbus State Community College. Su can be found hiking, frolicking in woods and gardens, exploring as many interesting old buildings and peculiar landmarks as possible, dancing around a lot, and being consistently awestruck by how many utterly delightful and fascinating experiences exist in this world. Su Flatt has performed poetry nationally as well as published poems in a variety of journals and 'zines.

Forrest Gander was born in the Mojave Desert and raised in Virginia. A translator/writer with degrees in geology and literature, he's received the Pulitzer Prize, Best Translated Book Award, and fellowships from the Library of Congress, Guggenheim, and US Artists Foundations. His book *Twice Alive* focuses on human and ecological intimacies. In 2024, New Directions will bring out his long poem on the desert, *Mojave Ghost*.

Audrey Gidman is a queer poet and workshop facilitator living in Maine. Her chapbook *body psalms* (Slate Roof Press, 2023) received the Elyse Wolf Prize. Her poems can be found in *Rust + Moth, Birdcoat Quarterly, The Night Heron Barks, SWWIM Every Day*, and elsewhere. Her reviews can be found in *DIAGRAM* and *The Inflectionist Review*, among others. She serves as a chapbook editor for Newfound.

Kari Gunter-Seymour, Poet Laureate of Ohio, authored *Alone in the House of My Heart* (2022) winner, Best Book Award, American Book Fest and *A Place So Deep Inside America It Can't Be Seen* (2020). Her work has been featured in *The New York Times, Verse Daily, World Literature Today*, and on *Poem-a-Day*. A ninth generation Appalachian, she is editor of *I Thought I Heard A Cardinal Sing: Ohio's Appalachian Voices*, and the Women of Appalachia Project's anthology series, *Women Speak*.

Lisa Hibl is the Director of the Russell Scholars Program at the University of Southern Maine. She studied literature at Bowdoin College and holds an MFA from Arizona State University and a PhD from Brandeis University. Her poems have appeared in *Black Fly Review, Hayden's Ferry Review, Hawaii Pacific Review, Untidy Candles: A Maine Poetry Anthology*, and the *Spoon River Anthology*. She recently contributed a chapter to *River Voices: Perspectives on the Presumpscot* (North Country Press, 2020).

Ryan Kegley lives in the Flint Hills outside Manhattan, Kansas where he works with Prairiewood, a tallgrass preserve. He was most recently published in *The New Territory* and was a 2023 Pushcart Prize nominee.

Stuart Kestenbaum, Maine's poet laureate (2016-21), authored six collections of poems, and *The View from Here* (Brynmorgen Press), a book of brief essays on craft and community. His poems and writing have appeared in *Tikkun, the Sun, the Beloit Poetry Journal,* and the *New York Times Magazine* among others. He hosted *Poems from Here* on Maine Public Radio/Maine Public Classical. He was the director of the Haystack Mountain School of Crafts for over 25 years.

Susan Landgraf received an Academy of American Poets Laureate Award in 2020, resulting in a book of Muckleshoot poetry from WSU. More than 400 of her poems have appeared in *Prairie Schooner, Poet Lore, Nimrod, Rattle* and others. Other books include *The Inspired Poet, What We Bury Changes the Ground, Other Voices,* and *Student Reflection Journal for Student Success.* A former journalist, she taught at Highline College for 30 years and at Shanghai Jiao Tong University.

Stacey Z Lawrence is a veteran teacher of Poetry & English at Columbia High School in New Jersey. Her poetry was short-listed for the Fish Prize in 2019/2021 & nominated for a Pushcart Prize in 2022. Stacey's first collection of poems, *Fall Risk* was released in August 2021 through Finishing Line Press.

Jill McCabe Johnson is the author of three poetry books and two chapbooks, and editor of three anthologies. Her most recent book is *Tangled in Vow & Beseech* (MoonPath, 2024), finalist in the Wheelbarrow Books and Sally Albiso Poetry Awards. Jill is editor-in-chief of Wandering Aengus Press. When not writing or editing, Jill can be found exploring the nearest trail. jillmccabejohnson.com

Jim Minick is the author or editor of 8 books, including *Without Warning: The Tornado of Udall, Kansas* (nonfiction), *The Intimacy of Spoons* (poetry, forthcoming), *Fire Is Your Water* (novel), and *The Blueberry Years: A Memoir of Farm and Family.* His work has appeared in many publications, including the *New York Times, Poets & Writers, Oxford American, Orion, Shenandoah, Appalachian Journal, Wind,* and *The Sun.* He serves as Coeditor of *Pine Mountain Sand & Gravel.*

Jefferson Navicky is the author of four books, most recently the novel-in-prose-poems, *Head of Island Beautification for the Rural Outlands* (2023), as well as *Antique Densities: Modern Parables & Other Experiments in Short Prose* (2021), which won the 2022 Maine Literary Book Award for Poetry. His work has appeared in *Smokelong Quarterly, Electric Literature, Fairy Tale Review, Southern Humanities Review,* and *Beloit Poetry Journal.* Jefferson works as the archivist for the Maine Women Writers Collection.

Patti Spady Ross' journalist work was first published in the *Washington Times* and the *Rural America* newspapers. She holds a certificate in Social Justice Writing from UC Berkeley and after a career in Technology is sharing her voice as the Spoken Word Artist "little pi." Her poems are published with PoetryXHunger, and in several journals and anthologies. Her debut chapbook is *St. Paul Street Provocations* (2021) the poem "Indemnity" was nominated for the Pushcart Prize. littlepisuniverse.com

Poet and creative collaborator **Linda Russo** explores ways of knowing and being in relationship with the more-than-human world. She is the author of three books of poems, including *Participant* and *Meaning to Go to the Origin in Some Way,* a book of essays, *To Think of Her Writing Awash in Light,* and co-editor of *Counter-Desecration: A Glossary for Writing Within the Anthropocene.* She lives on Nimíipuu and Pelúuc homelands and teaches at Washington State University where she directs EcoartsonthePalouse.com

Scott Woods is an Emmy award-winning writer and event organizer in Columbus, Ohio, and founder of Streetlight Guild. He authored 3 books and has been featured in national press, including National Public Radio. Awards include: Columbus Makes Art Excellence Award, Columbus Foundation Spirit of Columbus Award, Press Club of Cleveland's Ohio Excellence in Journalism. He is co-founder of the Writers' Block Poetry Night and the first poet to complete a 24-hour solo poetry reading.

Artists' Biographies

Martin Bridge (cover artist) carries his family tradition forth as he lives, creates and teaches in Western Massachusetts. His work spans: Drawing, Painting, Sculpture, Theater Design, Site Specific Installations, and Performance. As an avid Permaculture designer he strives to improve his awareness of how he relates to the natural world and to live in better balance. Through his work he hopes to inspire and cultivate a greater sense of mystery and possibility. thebridgebrothers.com

Marty Espinola is a retired educator who is also a widely published photographer. He wants to make use of the images he captures to benefit groups and individuals who care for the planet and each other. He still hopes we all have a chance if we work together. martyesp1@yahoo.com

About Lis McLoughlin (editor)

Lis McLoughlin, PhD is the founder and director of NatureCulture, through which she directs the Writing the Land Project; produces the online Authors and Artists festival/workshop at the intersection of arts, environment, and social justice; and holds annual international in-person retreats for environmental writers. Lis has degrees in Civil Engineering, Education, and Science and Technology Studies. She lives off-grid in Northfield, Massachusetts and part-time in Montréal, Québec.

About Patrick Curry (foreword author)

Patrick Curry is a Canadian-born writer and scholar who lives in London. He holds a PhD in the History and Philosophy of Science from University College London. He has been a Lecturer at the University of Kent and Bath Spa University, and remains a Tutor at the University of Wales Trinity St David. He is the author of *Defending Middle-Earth: Tolkien, Myth and Modernity*, rev ed. (2004), *Ecological Ethics: An Introduction*, rev. ed (2017), *Enchantment: Wonder in Modern Life* (2019) and most recently *Art and Enchantment: How Wonder Works* (2023). He is Editor-in Chief of *The Ecological Citizen* (ecologicalcitizen.net) and an Advisor to the Center for Climate Literacy and to Population Matters. patrickcurry.co.uk

Epilogue:
Accomack Spit, The Protected Land
by Forrest Gander

Introduction to the Epilgue: What Marks the Land Holds

The first dirt I tasted was a fistful of siltstone dust outside the house where I was born in the Mojave Desert. My father wasn't around much. When she could, my mother took long walks around the multicolored washes and canyons of Barstow's Rainbow Basin, now designated a National Natural Landmark. Her accounts of the changing light on the rock walls, of her encounters with silence and sidewinders, and her accumulating collection of fossils — including a broken camel rib and a piece of mastodon tooth plucked from sedimentary formations after rain — piqued my enthusiasm for earth science and led me to earn a degree in geology, the profession, it has been said, of those given to disinter memory.

History, as a geologist knows, is never far below the surface. The Chilean poet Raúl Zurita cannot look at the Chilean landscape without seeing the thousands of bodies that were dropped into the oceans and volcanoes from helicopters, that were burned and blown up in the Atacama Desert, and that were butchered with machetes during the brutal Pinochet regime. Along with rains, land absorbs and records footsteps and spilled blood and the various long histories that we no longer readily see when we look. Wherever we walk, we cross semi-permeable dimensions of time and space.

In this poem, I try to honor the complex registers of place. There are fractures and folds, metaphorical and real, beneath everywhere we take a stand.

Accomack Spit, The Protected Land
by Forrest Gander

Bay-facing scarps to the east
bound beds of yellow-orange
sand and sedge. And broken mollusk valves

stud the loamy fill in this paleochannel
of the Susquehanna. Pollen records tell
of pine, spruce, and birch— temperate days

following the violent whoomph
of a bolide that scooped out
Chesapeake Bay, leaving a crater

to fill first with seawater
and then fresh as hundreds of new rivers
gushed from the continent's mangled edge.

We're twenty miles south of Temperanceville, just
six from Modest Town, closer yet
to Gargatha, its name a corruption
of Aramaic Golgotha, "place of
skulls." Lackadaisical Parker Creek

curls through the marsh here,
and as the tide goes out,
the slick grey mud

of the creek's
bank is bared
like the gum of a snarling dog.

Below mudflats of cordgrass,
worms, pea clams, and small
crabs quiver in place, sludge-coated,
barely visible even to rails or the stalking
black-necked stilt. There beyond the dock,
where a dredged pocket of creek widens,

skimmers rake the surface and slo-mo
cattle-egrets wade the shallows and lesser
terns plunge headlong into brown, sun-warm water.

These dreaming, mosquito-riven sixty acres,
henceforth to be preserved intact,
were excised over years of inheritance and
sales from a larger tract of swamp
and high land that neighbored, to the northwest,
the plantation of one Benjamin West who found himself

On November 15, 1770 in a Court held in Accomack County
for the Examination of Moses Riggs on suspition of Murdering
a negro boy named Stepney Belonging to Benjamin West Junr.

Deponent Sarah Colony aged twenty one years or thereabouts
being sworn Saith that about nine o'clock in the morning
on Tuesday the ninth day of this Instant the said Moses the Prisoner
came to the house of Benjamin West the elder
with the Barrel of a Gun in his hand
which was Bloody and had Brains upon it
and said that Gun was Left him as a Legacy by his Daddy
and that he had killed the Devil with it
just Beyond Benjamin West the younger's fence
and thrown it in the roadside
and that there was his Blood and Brains Showing on his trowsers
and that she the Deponent went with Eliza. West the other witness
to where the sd. Moses said he had thrown the Devil
& saw the negro boy Stepney Lying with his head Beat all to Pieces
and the Brains in the road and Saw the But end of a Gun
and Several Broken pieces of Gun Stock Lying there
and that she saw a hole in the Body of the said negro
which answered to what the said Moses had said
that he Punched the Muzzle of the said Gun into his Body
until the Green Poison ran out. And this Deponent
saith that at the time Moses came & related the said Murder
he seemed to be much out of his senses
and further saith not.

Signed Sarah X Colony, her mark

Her mark preserved on the page
and on the land on which she lived. The land
which has always belonged to the land. History

is never far below the surface. Those people
have gone off. We see them
in our minds, but the sound is off. Our

listening fills in with fragments of our own story
while the soil swallows rain and gore, pesticides
and the incessant rupture of plows. This land—

inhabited by a religious people, planters and oystermen
and shoemakers. In October, Nelson's Sparrows flicker
through the marsh. Come winter, skeins of Brant

geese fly in from the east. Clapper rails, heard
more than seen. In the creek's meandering bends,
Southern two-lined salamanders breed in what we call

silence. Accomack, a quiet hamlet named
for the Accawmack Indians who presently comprise
.15 percent of the population.

I'd like to leave the violence behind.
Whoever thinks that they themselves
are the ones who commit the irrevocable?
Protecting these acres where
generations of families knew
happiness and felt connected to
each other, to the chafe
of grit between their toes, the
swamp-muck smell, the shrieks
of peacocks, is a good thing. I'd
like to honor the gesture of willing
this property into conservancy. It

cannot be subdivided and sold.
Still it's hard to overlook the report
of the first census in this county
when a third of the total population
was enslaved. I imagine I'm not unlike
the property owners then, thinking
there's nothing in me of moral blindness,
of the torturer's lust, of a self-
righteous conviction in the absolute
of my evangelical religion. A lapse
of judgement? I won't presume
to speak for others. I'm old enough
to also want to hold an image clear
from time's smudge. To propose
that a singular, seasonal orchestration
of birds and crickets and frogs play
on repeat. To sign my mark to an assurance
that what I remember won't disappear.
And then to sit back and admire the durable
allure of this place. But even on the un-
settled land I've come to call my own,
I sometimes feel a low tremor
beneath what it is I think
I stand on.

The protected property includes
a historic farmhouse, a second residence
called The Tree House. Supporting

structures include a horse barn,
storage buildings, a paddock, and a seafood kitchen
down near the dock on Parker Creek.

Milton Keynes UK
Ingram Content Group UK Ltd.
UKHW010816220424
441551UK00002B/262